Kim's story is one that is all too familiar to each and every one of us. It is filled with hurts and heartbreaks from the past to the present. It is also a story God desires His children to experience. He wants us to experience the true meaning of hurt turned into hope, and failure turned into faith, where joy comes in the morning. *God Had a Hand on Me* will encourage you as you read it. In each chapter you will begin to see clearly what the devil meant for harm, God used for good.

—Bryant Hemphill, pastor of Awaken Spokane

In Kim Dotson's fascinating new book, *God Had a Hand on Me: A Memoir about Pain, Healing, and Victory*, she shares her story of overcoming adversity, relational hardships, addictions, and difficult seasons only through the saving grace and power of her Lord and Savior, Jesus Christ. The doors the Lord opened for her are divine, inspiring, and truly amazing. Through personal story and biblical truth, this book brings a message of hope, freedom, and healing through a personal relationship with Jesus.

—Doris Swift, founder of Fierce Calling Ministries, host of the *Fierce Calling* podcast, and author of *Surrenderthe Joy Stealers: Rediscover the Jesus Joy in You*

Kim's story has a red thread running through it from beginning to end. As she reveals her story, the redemption blood of Christ is evident, proving all things do work for the good of those who love the Lord. God's love and glory shine brightly through Kim's story. A must-read for all who need hope in seeing God at work in their lives as well.

—Bonnie Chung, speaker and writer

God Had a Hand on Me is a moving narrative that tackles complex and sensitive issues with grace and authenticity. Through its pages, readers will find a resilient story of triumph in an honest account of hard life situations transformed to glorious through the redemptive work of Jesus Christ. This book is a testament to the power of vulnerability, self-discovery, and enduring hope.

—BJ Garrett, motivational speaker, author of *Unwanted No More: From Exploited to Embraced by God*

Kim's journey through abandonment, racial injustice, and her own rebellion is a witness to the redemptive power of our Lord and Savior, Jesus Christ. As she takes you by the hand and invites you gently along her painful path filled with grief and loss, she allows you to feel a small portion of her deep emotional journey, all the while leading you to the only place we can truly lay it all down and be made whole. You will cry for her losses. You will cheer for her wins. But most importantly, you will be reminded that redemption and forgiveness are found only at the foot of the cross.

—Pam Mitchael, speaker, writer, storyteller: *We Get You!: 30 Days • 30 Women • 30 Stories • One God*

God Had a Hand on Me is the perfect title for this book. A great read. Kim shares how God has been evident in every turn in her life, and when we lean into Christ, He will show us the way and lead us to victory (not exactly like we may think, but the best way to victory).

—Elizabeth Howell, author of *A Dream Come True: Finding Unwavering Faith on the Road to Parenthood*

From the very beginning, Kim grabs your heart with the tragic story of abandonment and experiences of racial prejudices. Her vulnerability to share how she not only repeats the devastating pattern but throughout her life falls again and again only magnifies the redeeming power of the Holy Spirit. Kim highlights biblical characters whose stories shaped her faith walk and gave her hope. If you are feeling unqualified, unseen, and unwanted, Kim's story of the life-changing grace of our living Lord will give you hope.

—Peg Arnold, speaker, author, drama queen for Christ

God

A Memoir

Had A

About Pain, Healing,

Hand

and Victory

On Me

God

A Memoir

Had A

About Pain, Healing,

Hand

and Victory

On Me

Kim Dotson

Published by Redemption Press Express, an imprint of Redemption Press, PO Box 427, Enumclaw, WA 98022. Toll-Free (844) 2REDEEM (273-3336)

Redemption Press Express is honored to present this title in partnership with the author. The views expressed or implied in this work are those of the author. Redemption Press Express provides our imprint seal representing design excellence, creative content, and high-quality production.

The author has tried to recreate events, locales, and conversations from memories of them. In order to maintain their anonymity, in some instances the names of individuals, some identifying characteristics, and some details have been changed, such as physical properties, occupations, and places of residence.

All Scripture quotations in this publication are taken from the Holy Bible, New Living Translation, copyright © 1996, 2004, 2015 by Tyndale House Foundation. Used by permission of Tyndale House Publishers, Carol Stream, IL 60188. All rights reserved.

ISBN 13: 978-1-64645-354-2 (Hardcover)
ISBN 13: 978-1-64645-355-9 (Paperback)
ISBN 13: 978-1-64645-356-6 (e-Pub)

Library of Congress Catalog Card Number: 2023919933

Dedication

To Brad

You have been such a blessing to me. You are an answer to a prayer I didn't know I had. Thank you for supporting me in everything I do, and thank you for remaining faithful to God even during the most difficult times.

To Leslie Dawn

You are my miracle child and the friend I don't deserve. You bless my life in ways you may never know. Thank you for your forgiveness. I praise the God of heaven's armies for choosing you to be my daughter.

To Kale

You are my redemption child and my friend. God used you to reveal a purpose for my life. You are the gift I never would have imagined.

To Diane

Thank you for loving me and leading me to a relationship with the Lord back in 1992. I don't know where I would be without Him.

To Dad and Rosie

Thank you for always encouraging me to grow and for loving me just as I am. I love you both.

And to Mom, Poppy, and Dennis

Earth is only tolerable without you because of knowing that heaven holds you now.

Foreword

Kim's memoir describes a journey common to children whose parents come from different backgrounds. Her mother was white, and I am Indian. We were both Catholic, but our faith didn't overcome incongruent values. We met while attending junior college in Coeur d'Alene, Idaho, during the 1950s. Our young love challenged differences and social sanctions of our families as well as racism. We were poor, and the early years were very difficult. Our marriage was fraught with differences and anger. We never had enough money. Our lifestyle was typical of poor reservation Indians. Being indigenous is very expensive. Our dream grew into antecedents leading to separation and divorce.

I always believed in simple "cowboy logic." I loved western music, including spiritual songs. Jesus was prominent in many ways through the plethora of recordings I had collected.

An aspiring professional cowboy's life recently came apart, and he hit bottom hard. He pleaded in desperation, "Jesus, I need Your help; I don't know where to turn." That was not my experience. But I know that Jesus is always ready. I know He helps people who need Him. Kim is one of those people. She has worked hard at being a medical provider to help people, doing the work God chose for her. She describes that path in her book, a story you will find most intriguing. God bless Kim and everyone who reads her story.

~ R.C. Covington, Kim's father

Preface

On December 8, 2017, at 7:10 a.m., God gave me the title of a book, along with the names of several chapters. I recorded all of it in the Notes section on my phone. I knew God had spoken into my life and was revealing His calling to me.

While some people might prefer to hide the ugliness that sin creates in their lives, I am sharing my truth because I recognize God allows everything to happen for a reason. He has intentionally placed certain people in my path to accomplish His purpose in my life and in theirs. My story will also reveal how God appointed others to touch my life for His glory.

I find myself in awe of God's grace when I have an opportunity to share bits of my personal narrative with others, describing how He has intervened on my behalf. Despite many hardships, I am confident I am right where God has placed me for His divine purposes. This literary journey has taken me back to some dark moments in my life. But I have come through with a better understanding of God's purpose for allowing some of the challenges and personal hardships I faced. He used these challenges to grow me into a better version of myself.

I am called to act in obedience. It's a theme God has written on my heart. I hope my testimony speaks to you and God's gracious, merciful love is glorified through it. If you are walking through pain, perhaps God has you reading this for a reason. I hope you go with it. I pray everyone who reads this book experiences an encounter with God. We all have a story; this is mine.

I am adding this disclaimer: A part of my story reveals how I ended up forfeiting formal education at a young age. At one point in this venture, I asked my niece (someone whom I trust and adore) to proofread my manuscript. One morning in church I believe God whispered something to me. He said the way I tell my story depicts a part of my journey. God knows all my faults, fears, and failures, and He loves me anyway. He wants my authenticity, so I am pressing on with the raw, unretouched version of my truth.

I also have a confession. I thought my story was ready to be shared in 2022, but during a study of Genesis my perspective changed. God impressed upon my heart an immeasurably valuable lesson. As I came to know the people of the Old Testament, I read about Jacob's son Joseph. I was astounded by the grace he extended to his brothers. After all, they sold him into slavery, basically exiling him to Egypt. He was separated from his family, and during that time he was imprisoned unfairly. While he was alone and destitute, his brothers unapologetically moved on without him in an act of ultimate deception.

Despite Joseph's situation, God blessed his life with great favor. Over twenty years later, when he was finally reunited with his family, Joseph openly acknowledged their detestable actions without exercising resentment. He humbly offered forgiveness, telling them God allowed everything to happen to save all of them from the famine. Joseph's painful but victorious story glorifies God inexplicably.

God used this story of forgiveness to impress on my heart an immeasurably valuable lesson. During my writing, I recognized myself experiencing and reliving hurts from the past. In my painful state, a part of me wanted to inflict a little pain myself. I wanted to expose those who had hurt me. But that was my sin nature, which was not God's purpose for this book.

God reminded me it is okay to acknowledge actions that may have hurt me, but I am called to extend grace to others, just as He extends grace to me. In Christ I am a new creation. I am no longer the little girl who saw herself as abandoned but a child of the King.

God revealed some changes He wanted me to make. Ultimately, the purpose of the book is to demonstrate how God's hand has been upon me throughout my life. It is about the good He has done in my life, not the bad inflicted by others. To focus on the bad serves to glorify the work of the enemy.

I removed the harmful words I had written. Nothing in my story now is intended to hurt, shame, blame, or destroy. It's about redemption. I hope you experience healing and redemption through my pain.

To God be the glory!

Contents

Acknowledgments

Thank you to my Lord and Savior, Jesus Christ, for blessing me with the riches of eternity in heaven—not because of anything I have done but because of Your loving mercy and grace.

Thank you to my project manager, Christina England, my managing editor, Kathy Ide, and the whole team at Redemption Press Express/ Redemption Press. From day one you guided me to success, encouraging me along the way. You helped me find my "other" tribe at the Christian Communicators Conference, and for that I am forever blessed.

Humble thanks to my extraordinary editor, Ken Walker. You are such a blessing in my life. You honored my truth and helped me share it in the best way possible. There are no chance meetings, and I am so grateful God chose you to help me on this part of my journey.

Thank you to my prayer team: Colleen, Kristina, Deb, Leslie Dawn, Judy, Millie, and Nancy. We all need people who are willing to stand beside us when we go into battle for the Lord. I appreciate your faithfulness in accompanying me through this one.

Thank you to Bree for encouraging me to go further than I otherwise would have with my story. There is always more to tell.

Chapter 1

Haunting Memories

More than fifty years later, my memories of the day my parents divorced still haunt me. Dad picked up my siblings and me that afternoon in front of St. Thomas School and told us he had "won us" in court. The scene unfolds in my mind as if I were another person watching this painful memory transpire. I can visualize the playground behind me as I stepped off the curb, though I was only in second grade then. I am still saddened by the tragedy I experienced.

I climbed into the back seat as my father shared the news that his marriage to Mom had ended. From that point on it would be me, my little brother, my big sister, and Dad making our way in the world. My brother and sister were my very first friends. My father instructed the three of us from an early age that we were to always stick up for each other, no matter what.

I have fond memories of us playing in and around the towering weeping willow in our backyard. Its roots peeked through the earth as they extended on all sides beneath that grand old tree, which is a metaphor for the person I am today. Reflecting on our neighborhood games of hide-and-seek on warm summer evenings, and sledding on moonlit nights down a closed street with my siblings, make me long for simpler times.

There are painful memories too. Like the heartbreaking scene that materialized the night of our parents' divorce. We three little children sat on the living room floor in our pajamas. Despite the news from earlier in the day, we were doing what kids do: watching cartoons and our favorite game show, *The Price Is Right*. Mom showed up at the front door, intoxicated, grieving her loss. Her tears and mourning made me feel awkward and uncomfortable.

Her maroon-tinted hair was tucked back in a chignon above the midnight fur collar of her light-blue overcoat. Her Interlude perfume hung heavy in the air, transfused with the aroma of whiskey and cigarettes.

Between coarse sobs she asked my father to hold her, but he refused. With us youngsters sitting at their feet, the raw emotions our parents displayed were palpable. My mother's guttural cry echoed on the chambers of my heart. I had no way of understanding everything that had transpired between them, and I will never know all the details, but I know there was a lot of pain. And shame. It was not mine to carry, but I carried it anyway.

Years later I learned that my mother never forgave herself for the pain she caused by leaving us for another man. She did the best she could at the time, but my heart remains deeply scarred because of her indiscretion. I am flawed with insecurities, fearful of rejection and abandonment, and poorly equipped to manage disappointment. From a young age, I've felt burdened with an insatiable need to create my own validity in a world that often showed me just how disposable I am.

Despite the angst buried deep within my desolation, God's Word tells me His power is made perfect in my weakness. My life is a testimony of this truth from the Lord: "My grace is all you need. My power works best in weakness" (2 Cor. 12:9). Yet at the time, I carried a burden of shame for things over which I had no control, especially the fact that my parents were divorced (at a time when divorce was not so common), and then both remarried. I suffered immense sadness, loneliness, and yearning for my mother's touch because we were separated by two hundred miles.

I cringed when I had to explain to my friends why I called my stepmother by her first name instead of Mom. If I had known at the time that my mother left her three children to build a life with the man she later married, I would have been ashamed of that too. Instead, I was simply ashamed of myself.

> Despite the angst buried deep within my desolation, God's word tells me his power is made perfect in my weakness.

I was ashamed of being half Indian and half white. I grew up in the 1970s in a home where it seemed white people were not revered. Today I recognize there were some valid reasons for that sentiment, as both my father and stepmother have lifelong experiences with the profound ugliness of racism. I would say it was the norm of the day, but unfortunately, racism still exists in America. In fact, despite modern efforts to promote inclusivity, the separation and hatred resulting from racism seem to be alive in our midst now more than ever.

Most people of color can relate, regardless of where they live. I recently read a memoir by Michael Fuller called Kill the Black One First. In it, Britain's first Black chief constable shares how he was accused of being overly sensitive when he voiced objections to fellow officers referring to Black people using unfriendly and despised terminology. I can identify, having been accused of being overly sensitive when speaking up after friends casually stated they "sat Indian style" or called a work meeting a "powwow." Throughout my life I have been called names like "injun," "squaw," and "redskin" and dealt with war whoops announcing my presence.

My siblings and I were the only half–Native American students attending our school in Missoula. We were raised to be proud of our heritage, but not everyone valued it like we did.

As I walked home from school one day, an older kid made fun of me for being Indian. At home, I collapsed in tears. My father volunteered to give a talk at my school to educate the students about Native Americans. My brother helped him set up a small teepee, and he brought several artifacts for the students to explore while he shared his talk. He titled it "Everything You Wanted to Know about Indians But Were Afraid to Ask."

Despite the occasional indignities, we celebrated our heritage. Summertime in our family often meant traveling to powwows around Montana and the Pacific Northwest, where we camped under the stars and participated in traditional Native dancing. We ate stew and frybread from the food stands and ran around in preadolescent packs with our cousins. I stood with my grandparents as stick game players sang late into the night.

When a well-known emcee announced the drum and beckoned dancers over the loudspeaker, "Intertribal—everybody dance!" my little brother likened this invitation to a gun going off at the start of a race. It was his signal to take off and complete the dance circle as many times as possible. He skipped as

> **Summertime in our family often meant traveling to pow wows around Montana and the Pacific Northwest, where we camped under the stars and participated in traditional Native dancing.**

quickly as he could (his juvenile but competitive form of dancing). To him it was a race to be won. He looked so cute in his regalia!

For many years my brother was the only boy among several cousins. When the girls gathered in the bathroom for makeup and girl talk, he stood in the hall alone, begging us to let him in and promising not to look. My great-grandma T'upia (we called her Toopie) endearingly called him Wheet Su'taah. We called him Charging Buzzard.

All my experiences played an integral part in forming the person I am today. They remain deeply embedded in my core, reminding me of the rich culture bonding my people to the earth. I embrace them, even those that hurt.

The Johari Window model was developed in the mid-1950s by two psychologists as a way to improve understanding and communication among members of a group. It's based on the idea that trust can be acquired by revealing information about yourself to others and learning about yourself from their feedback.

The Johari Window contains four panes: two represent self, and the other two represent the part unknown to self but known to others.

One of those panes is the "hidden area," those things we keep private about ourselves for various reasons. For me, sharing may open a door for someone who has a similar story, and it may offer that person hope for healing. If a loving God could heal and restore me, why not you too?

Chapter 2

Being Different

In the aftermath of Mom and Dad's divorce, we moved to the college town of Missoula, Montana. Fear and sadness were my companions as we traveled over the treacherous mountain pass during the winter break in 1970.

I was nine years old when we moved all our belongings two hundred miles away from my closest friends, cousins, and mother to start a new life in Big Sky Country. The road was a solid snowpack, and I lay in the back seat with my eyes closed, hoping my new hat and mittens would stay on to keep me warm if we ran off the road. I prayed silently that God would keep us safe.

In the middle of third grade, I started a new chapter in my life. A girl named Patti welcomed me as I entered my new classroom at Hawthorne Elementary School wearing my fluffy white faux fur coat. We became instant friends.

Hawthorne was a public school, a change from the parochial school I attended in first and second grades. In that Catholic environment I had learned about Jesus. I knew how to genuflect and when it was time to kneel or stand during mass. I could recite the Lord's Prayer and say my Hail Marys perfectly. To the world I looked like a good little Christian. But looks can be deceiving.

At my new school I was the same person, but I dressed differently. Instead of a uniform, I wore jeans like everyone else.

Here, talk of God didn't roll naturally off everyone's lips—except for Patti's. On the outside she looked like a regular kid, but she had a heart for Jesus. She shared her faith with me. And her warm, loving family welcomed me into their home.

Patti looked like a delicate little blond ballerina. She had an amazing collection of unique dolls. She told me only a certain number of each doll was made before they "broke the mold." In my naivete, I envisioned a hammer crushing the molds to smithereens, leaving a deep impression of how rare and special those dolls were. I knew I would never own one.

I felt blessed to have Patti as a friend because she had something even more valuable than her dolls. She had Jesus, and I needed Him desperately—I just didn't know it yet. I wouldn't recognize it for nearly twenty-five years. Yet I now see my childhood friendship with Patti as evidence of God working in my life, even at a young age.

Cruel Words

At that school in Missoula, the kids became like a family to me. Like most schools in our community at the time, it was a small institution covering kindergarten through eighth grade. I looked up to the older students, and I couldn't wait to be an eighth grader myself, hoping to become some sort of role model.

In fourth grade, I experienced a defining moment in my life. I stood in line on the playground, waiting to go back into school after playing foursquare and tetherball during recess. A girl near me wore turquoise pants and a matching sweater that accentuated her tiny waist. With her luxurious curls, her hair was the envy of most girls in my class. She had siblings who attended our school.

This girl, whom I'd considered my friend, looked at me and called me a "dirty little Indian."

Her words stung like venom. Did she truly see me as dirty and little in comparison to her? We were the same size, but "little" seemed to imply I bore less significance. Using "dirty" and "little" together created a vision in my mind of a cast-aside urchin with no value.

> This girl, whom I'd considered my friend, looked at me and called me a "dirty little Indian."

Did the expression come from her family's teaching? Perhaps it was like calling someone an idiot—just a random insult that meant little and was only intended to make the recipient feel bad.

Was I being overly sensitive? Maybe. All I knew at the time was that I had been defined in a three-word phrase. And I would never forget the feelings those words invoked.

Getting Over the Past

Regardless of what that girl meant, thought, or believed about me, life-long damage was done that day. At more than sixty years of age, I can still hear them as plain as the day she uttered them. She probably has no recollection of the event.

That incident when I was ten represents only a miniscule leg of my journey, but it stole more of my life than those three careless words were worth. For several years after, I accepted it as truth, absorbed it as a part of my biography, and believed it deep within my soul. I became the little urchin who felt kicked aside by life. I tried harder in everything I did to somehow gain my way into acceptance, importance, and value.

I suppose the insult served me well ultimately because I refused to give up.

As I postulate on those scarring words, my adult brain recognizes that children can be thoughtless and they often say mean things. I forgave the deed long ago. The shame is long gone now. I know that I am neither dirty nor little. I am a human being, created in the likeness of God!

The sentiment depicted through those careless words now stirs a desire within me to right the wrongs of the injustice of racism.

The enemy used words to harm me. But I am not that little girl anymore. Today I exercise my voice when it comes to racially ignorant comments. I am called to use the talents God has given me to speak truth and shed light where the enemy tries to divide people based on their God-designed differences.

We are all created in His image. We are called to love one another and to celebrate our uniqueness, because we are made new in Christ. As Ephesians 2:14–16 says:

> We are all created in His image. We are called to love one another and to celebrate our uniqueness because we are made new in Christ.

Christ himself has brought peace to us. He united Jews and Gentiles into one people when, in his own body on the cross, he broke down the wall of hostility that separated us. He did this by ending the system of law with its commandments and regulations. He made peace between Jews and Gentiles by creating in himself one new people from the two groups. Together as one body, Christ reconciled both groups to God, by means of his death on the cross, and our hostility toward each other was put to death.

Treasured Memories

Although I haven't lived in Montana since I was fourteen, I still consider it my home. Our first residence there was a duplex about a block from my school. Patti lived close by, and we often walked to and from school together. After school we played with her Barbies in her bedroom, which was enormous and beautiful compared to the room I shared with my brother and sister.

Our bedroom contained a set of bunkbeds and my brother's bed, all jammed together. When he grew a little older, my father created a space for my brother in our garage. It was heated and actually quite comfortable.

Patti had her own upstairs bedroom with her very own window that overlooked her front yard, just like a princess. Everything about her house seemed magical, from her bedroom furniture to the backyard forest where we could escape to a land of make-believe.

In my mind, Patti lived a fairy-tale life. Her parents were happily married, which left a lasting impression on me. To this day, her parents live in that same house and remain together. My father and stepmother have been married for fifty-plus years now, but my naivete led me to believe I was "less than" because my parents had divorced.

A few years ago, I saw Patti's mother when I ran my annual half-marathon. I cried as I hugged her. She was just as I had remembered! Patti recalls the winter I arrived different than I do. Unbeknownst to me, the teacher had announced there would be a new girl in class: an Indian. Patti couldn't wait for me to arrive and befriend me. She felt special because she had an Indian friend.

I never considered my Indianness special. Honestly, it often felt more like a burden. I was never just me, but always "that Indian girl."

Despite my self-loathing, I was an exceptional student. I loved to read, and I studied hard to prove my worth and be my best. Even though I felt insignificant, God blessed me with wisdom, a strong desire to learn, and the self-discipline to maintain good grades.

He also blessed me with opportunities to excel in team sports. Despite some of the slurs from thoughtless classmates, I was well liked. Because I looked different, I stood out. God used my uniqueness to set me up for success. It has always been His plan for me.

But I also have an adversary who wants to destroy me.

Attempting to Assimilate

When I was in seventh grade, we moved to a reservation in southeastern Montana for one year. Ironically, I became recognized and challenged because of my "whiteness." The white kids didn't accept me as one of them, and the Indian kids shunned me as well. I was an outsider no matter where I went.

I often heard my parents speak about their experiences with white people, and they were not always positive. Of course, I knew they were not referring to me or my siblings, but we were, after all, half white. I absorbed the negative sentiments. I felt "less than" at home because I was half white; I felt "less than" in the world because I was half Indian.

At the time this experience was painful. But God uses everything for our good. I believe He was preparing me for my future life as a Christian. I am a foreigner on this earth, longing for my heavenly home. My Father created me for something better than this world has to offer.

I am merely passing through a world that is only temporary. Here in this life, I am constantly attempting to assimilate, overlooking the insensitive comments of others. But this olive-toned earth suit that holds my soul is temporary. It's significantly insignificant, because one day it will be gone.

Being different on the outside does not make me "less than"; it makes me me. I am beautifully and wonderfully made. I am an example of God's

> **Being different on the outside does not make me "less than"; it makes me *me*.**

handiwork, and I am not a mistake. He created me to be all that I am. I know the Creator of the universe and everything in it, and He hears me when I speak to Him. I know this because He answers me.

God has placed people in my life who need to hear how verbal injustice has made me stronger. He has allowed me to come into relationships with people who listen when I say I will not tolerate any form of racism from anyone. God has given me a voice to speak against the bias of racism because I have painfully walked in it, carried the burden, nursed the wounds, and emerged victorious.

Chapter 3

Learning Racism

As much as that girl's "dirty little Indian" remark in fourth grade wounded me, I have to confess to engaging in similar behavior just three years later.

During my year on the reservation, a white family with three daughters lived near us. As ashamed as I am to admit it, I made fun of them and bullied them simply because of the color of their skin.

Why would I engage in the same kind of behavior that had hurt me so badly? I'm half white. Punishing white people was essentially self-abhorrence. Was I just being mean because seventh graders are typically mean?

At that age I certainly didn't think it through. But name-calling, stereotyping, and categorizing someone for the color of their skin, their ethnic background, or other characteristics is simply hatred. There is no reason or justification for it.

In the 1970s I responded to Indian slurs by calling my detractors "stupid honkeys." (I don't use that phrase any longer, of course.) As a paramedic in Spokane, Washington, I commonly heard coworkers refer to a drunk Native American as AFDI: "another (expletive) drunk Indian." Such stereotyping is cruel and heartless.

I wonder if people who participate in the "tomahawk chop" at sporting events have ever considered how this action appears to someone like me. Or whether people who argue that it's important to keep statues of great Americans who marginalized others "in the "name of history" have any regard for the pain their actions caused for those they harmed and the descendants who followed. Racism is insidious. It's everywhere, not just in American history but throughout the annals of time. The Jews hated the Samaritans and the Gentiles. It's been around forever. But it's still wrong.

I wince when I recall the times in my life when I participated in racist behavior. I was like a chameleon, adapting to my surroundings. While I understand the experiences that led me to behave this way, I cannot excuse or defend my actions.

Today I recognize a call to do better than adapt. In my heavenly Father's house, all are welcome, celebrated, and loved. I want my identity to be a Christ follower, an image bearer of the King.

> God's love has no color. All are created in His image, and all have sinned and fallen short of His glory.

God's love has no color. All are created in His image, and all have sinned and fallen short of His glory. I am no better than anyone. I am a sinner in need of a Savior, just like everyone else. It may have taken more than forty years for me to recognize God's handiwork, but He completes every good work He starts in a person. If we expectantly watch and patiently listen, we will see His hand in everything and recognize His voice.

Returning Home

After one year in southeastern Montana, my family returned to our old neighborhood. During our time away, a fire burned down our beloved school—everything but the gymnasium. As a result, my siblings and I were bused to the annex of another school. Although in new surroundings, I felt comfortable because I was back among friends. But I had changed during my time away.

On the reservation I'd developed an interest in cigarettes and alcohol. Our mother smoked, and cigarettes were easily accessible in her kitchen drawer. Although she lived two hundred miles away, after the divorce we spent summers with her.

Mom worked the night shift, and one summer she hired an older lady named Peggy to care for us. Since Peggy couldn't keep up with us, we sort of ran all over her. We regularly stayed awake late into the night, and that's when we first experimented with smoking.

I started drinking alcohol the summer between seventh and eighth grade, throwing a curveball at my still-developing nervous system. Satan likely celebrated.

I was making terrible decisions. If I could reach back to stop myself, I would at least try. But God uses everything in our lives, including our stupid mistakes.

Things went awry between me and Patti, and by eighth grade we were no longer friends. Like the cliché says, "Hurt people hurt people." I was so mean to Patti and her friends that toward the end of our eighth-grade year, she wrote and recited a speech titled "Popular Versus Unpopular." Her speech called me out, and consequently I lashed out at her.

A few years ago, God allowed me to reconnect with her. I apologized for the pain I caused her all those years ago, and we built a loving adult friendship. Our faith is a big part of our relationship today. God blessed us with healing and restoration, demonstrating His promise to complete every good work.

Satanic Strongholds

My brokenness developed into self-abhorrence and shame, which became strongholds that Satan used to try to harm me. Feeling abandoned, I internalized my pain by labeling myself as unlovable.

But God provided healing, joy, and redemption. He even used shame and abandonment as the building blocks of strength, compassion, and encouragement. A promise fulfilled! As Isaiah 61:3 says, "To all who mourn in Israel, he will give a crown of beauty for ashes, a joyous blessing instead of mourning, festive praise instead of despair. In their righteousness, they will be like great oaks that the Lord has planted for his own glory."

> **Today I know God sees me. There is power and healing behind that statement.**

Today I know God sees me. There is power and healing behind that statement.

The Bible illustrates this through the story of Hagar, an Egyptian servant. Abram's wife, Sarai, gave Hagar to Abram after years of heartbreaking barrenness. When Hagar became pregnant, she developed contempt for Sarai. Sarai blamed Abram for Hagar's behavior. Both Sarai and Abram hurt Hagar. Feeling dejected, Hagar ran away. But God sent an angel to instruct her to return to her mistress. He promised Hagar more descendants than she could count.

Though she was hurt by Abram and Sarai, God blessed her. "Thereafter, Hagar used another name to refer to the Lord, who had spoken to her. She said, 'You are the God who sees me.' She also said, 'Have I truly seen the One who sees me?'" (Gen. 16:13).

Just as God saw Hagar, Jesus saw a Samaritan woman during a time and in a culture where women were not valued. Especially Samaritans, the "halfbreeds" to whom Jews didn't even speak. Yet Jesus intentionally made a detour to Samaria to reveal Himself to this woman as she drew water from a historic well. Jesus knew her story, and His encounter with her demonstrates that He is a very personal God.

This Samaritan woman was considered "less than" by many around her. After all, she had been divorced five times and was an adulteress living in wedlock with another man. She was shunned by everyone. Yet Jesus met with her personally at Jacob's well. Her encounter with Jesus was so profound, she ran back to town, forgetting the purpose of her trip—to collect the precious resource of fresh water. "The woman left her water jar beside the well and ran back to the village, telling everyone, 'Come and see a man who told me everything I ever did! Could he possibly be the Messiah?'" (John 4:28–29).

I can identify with that woman. While pain is part of my story, I believe telling it can bring hope and strength to others who struggle with feelings of shame and abandonment. When we feel unseen and unheard by the world, the God of the universe offers healing. He sees us. He hears our cries. And He can make beauty from ashes.

Chapter 4

The Rooster Crowed

My family is mostly Roman Catholic; my mother and father grew up in families who embraced their experience with God through Catholicism. In first and second grade, I went to the school my mother and grandmother attended as children. My sister and I wore the same blue plaid uniform jumpers to school they did, while my brother donned the familiar white shirt with a clip-on tie and salt-and-pepper corduroy trousers.

Another parochial school tradition featured obediently gathering every morning around the flagpole outside the school to honor the flag with the Pledge of Allegiance. One autumn morning this rite turned into an embarrassing ritual.

With a newly divorced father overseeing first-, second-, and third-grade youngsters, we often struggled to get out of the house in a timely manner. Despite the power-packed 383 V-8 engine in Dad's plum-colored 1970 Dodge Super Bee, we arrived late that day and missed the group recitation. The principal scolded us at the flagpole in front of the entire student body. How embarrassing!

Later that year, the principal humiliated me again. During a weekend at my cousins' house, I discovered the craft of beading. My first project was a medallion, and I worked on it meticulously for hours. I pinned it on my school uniform in a proud display of my ancestry, culture, and newfound skill.

Instead of expressing admiration for my project, the principal called me to the front of the room and chastised me for breaking the rule against accessorizing our uniforms. At her insistence, I tearfully tossed it in the garbage.

As I spent time with the Lord recently, He revealed to me the possible reason for the principal's action. She may have had good intentions, but not giving me any explanation inflicted a meaningless and painful lesson. However, God wastes nothing.

He led me to read Exodus 32. The Israelites were impatiently waiting for Moses to come down from Mount Sinai, where he had been speaking with God. They implored Aaron to make them some gods who could lead them, then handed him their earrings. Aaron melted them down and molded the gold into the shape of a calf. When the people saw it, they worshipped the idol. In their minds, an object they could hold in their hands was more valuable than a word from the Lord.

Reason for Rule

While I remain unsettled about what I saw as bullying behavior from a school principal, God revealed to me the reason for the rule. My little medallion and the culture it represented might have set me apart from others. But in my principal's eyes, the little beaded artifact could be a distraction—a type of golden calf—and therefore should not be celebrated. We are to offer our wholehearted worship to God, not material things.

God used this scenario to teach me about idol worship. At a time when individualization is embraced, celebrated, and revered in American culture, it is important to remember that our respect and admiration should always be directed toward God. Pride, ego, materialism, social status, worldly knowledge, money, and self-image distract us from a proper focus on what is lasting and valuable.

> At a time when individualization is embraced, celebrated, and revered in American culture, it is important to remember that our respect and admiration should always be directed toward God.

At the end of my second-grade year, that parochial school closed. All the teachers moved back to Pennsylvania, as did the principal, while my family moved to Spokane, Washington. At the public school we attended there, we could wear whatever we wanted. We no longer had to participate in daily mass or gather around the flagpole every morning.

My family pretty much only attended church on Christmas Eve and Easter, and even then it was hit-and-miss.

I received my first communion with my cousin at summer catechism classes on the reservation. My aunt made me a simple but beautiful pale-blue, tulle, daisy-motif dress for the ceremony. After receiving the elements, I sang "He's Got the Whole World in His Hands" at the top of my lungs. But I didn't know Christ.

When I was a teenager, another aunt led a series of weekend discipleship classes in her home to prepare several of my cousins for Catholic confirmation. This seemed like something I should do, but I was not seeking a relationship with Jesus. Nothing transpired within my heart. I simply went through the motions, exercising religious piety, checking a box.

Story of Betrayal

The aunt who taught those classes gave me a cloisonné lapel pin. Just over an inch in diameter, it was a blue, yellow, and red rooster with gold trim. With it, she told me the story from the New Testament where Jesus predicted Peter's betrayal. "I tell you the truth, Peter—this very night, before the rooster crows, you will deny three times that you even know me" (Matt. 26:34).

Peter insisted it would never happen. When it did, shame filled him and he wept bitterly. He probably recalled their conversation during what was to be the Last Supper with Jesus, where Jesus said to Peter (known then as Simon):

I have pleaded in prayer for you, Simon, that your faith should not fail. So when you have repented and turned to me again, strengthen your brothers."
Peter said, "Lord, I am ready to go to prison with you, and even to die with you."
But Jesus said, "Peter, let me tell you something. Before the rooster crows tomorrow morning, you will deny three times that you even know me. (Luke 22:32–34)

Later that evening Jesus went to the Mount of Olives to pray. The Bible says He was troubled. He told Peter and the sons of Zebedee His soul was overwhelmed with sorrow to the point of death. Jesus fell to the ground and prayed fervently, asking God to take away the cup of suffering. Verse 44 describes his sweat as akin to "great drops of blood." Three times he did this. Each time when he returned, He found His disciples sleeping.

Knowing what He was about to face, Jesus pleaded with God, asking if there was some other way to accomplish payment for the penalty of a crime He didn't commit (our sins). Yet Jesus remained obedient and submitted to God.

Meanwhile, His disciples slept. In His hour of need Jesus was abandoned by the people He should have been able to count on.

Soon after, a crowd approached. As the Lord had prophesied, Judas betrayed Him with a kiss. Jesus was arrested and taken to the courts, where people spat on Him. A fearful Peter hid in the shadows, watching.

Luke 22:56–59 describes how a servant girl looked at Peter and identified him as one of Jesus's followers. He steadfastly denied it. This happened two more times, ending with Peter's declaration, "Man, I don't know what you are talking about." While he was still speaking, a rooster crowed. At that moment Jesus looked at Peter. Suddenly, His words flashed through Peter's mind: "Before the rooster crows tomorrow morning, you will deny three times that you even know me" (vv. 60–61).

> "Before the rooster crows tomorrow morning you will deny three times that you even know me."

Can you imagine how Peter must have felt at that moment? It's no wonder he wept bitterly.

Heartfelt Lesson

The story of this dramatic encounter was embedded deeply in my heart that day.

Fast-forward thirty-five years. Family politics and strife had placed a wedge between me and the aunt who gave me that pin. In bitterness, I chose to hold a grudge against her. We hadn't spoken more than a few words to each other for a decade when she became very ill.

God put a burden on my heart to go to her on several occasions, but I couldn't bring myself to do it and found excuses to avoid her. In truth, I feared rejection and couldn't face the possibility of another hurtful incident. The childhood abandonment I experienced led me to build walls around my heart to protect myself from the pain inflicted by the people closest to me.

About three weeks later, I received a call that my aunt had passed away. At that instant, I heard a rooster crow in my soul, heart, and mind. I had denied the Holy Spirit's nudge, and my opportunity had passed forever. I understood completely what Peter's grief, shame, and regret must have felt like.

As much anguish as I experienced, though, I found hope in the rest of Peter's story. John 21:4–19 relates events a week after Jesus died a horrible death on the cross. Still reeking of shame, Peter had returned to his life as a fisherman, along with some of the other disciples. After spending an entire night on the Sea of Galilee, their nets came back empty.

Jesus called to them from the beach, though they didn't recognize Him. He asked if they had caught any fish, and they replied, "No." He told them to throw their net on the right side of the boat. When they did, their nets contained so many fish they couldn't haul them in.

Suddenly Peter recognized the Lord. He put on his tunic, jumped into the water, and swam to shore. When the others managed to get the boat and their impressive haul of fish to land, they found breakfast waiting: fish cooking on a charcoal fire and some bread.

This marked the third time Jesus had appeared to the disciples since His resurrection.

After breakfast, Jesus asked Peter a trio of questions, each including the phrase "Do you love me?" (vv. 15–17). When Peter insisted he did, the Lord gave him instructions to feed His lambs (His followers), take care of His sheep, and feed them. Then He prophesied about the fateful future Peter faced:

> When you were young, you were able to do as you liked; you dressed your-self and went wherever you wanted to go. But when you are old, you will stretch out your hands, and others will dress you and take you where you don't want to go." Jesus said this to let him know by what kind of death

he would glorify God. Then Jesus told him, "Follow me" (vv. 18–19). Peter, who had returned to fishing only to come back empty handed, was blessed with a net full of fish by the Lord he had denied three times. And for each denial, Peter had the opportunity to proclaim his love for Jesus. Thus, Peter was reinstated to his eternal purpose, which involved much more than fish. Jesus lovingly used Peter's personal circumstances to restore him so he would be equipped to accomplish his purpose. The Lord used Peter's shame and guilt for his good.

On the day of Pentecost, the gift Jesus had promised arrived. Peter and the other disciples were filled with the Holy Spirit. This empowered Peter with such bold faith he gave a speech proclaiming the good news of the gospel and encouraging people to repent and be baptized. Earlier that day there were only 120 followers of Jesus, but in response to Peter's sermon about three thousand people were baptized in the name of Jesus.

God uses even our failures to accomplish His good.

My guilt and shame over my disobedience at the moment I figuratively heard the rooster crow taught me a valuable lesson: There is a God in heaven who knows me personally. He uses the circumstances of my life to demonstrate His love for me in a way no human being ever could. Just as He used Peter's past to speak into his life, He used my mentor's faith many years ago to speak a story into my life that I would never forget.

> **God uses even our failures to accomplish his good.**

He also used her passing to gently illustrate the importance of obedience in following Him. God uses everything to demonstrate His ever-present hand upon me. Wow!

Chapter 5

Vivid Dreams

For several years, sleep brought me recurring visions of tornadoes. They all had a similar theme: my family and me surrounded by dark, ominous funnel clouds as far as the eye could see.

In one dream we found shelter under a stairwell. Another time we crouched beneath an underpass until the danger passed. Once, after we went down to the basement, we emerged to find that many of the walls surrounding us had been destroyed in the storm. We viewed the remains of our surroundings through gaping holes where concrete walls once stood.

As we stood amid the rubble, we felt awed by the devastation. Though amazed and bewildered, we did not experience fear.

In every dream, we always took shelter in a matter-of-fact, unhurried manner, lacking any sense of urgency, panic, or fear. We simply watched the storms twirl violently and majestically before us.

In one dream, I looked around as one funnel cloud after another swept over the horizon, and I marveled at them. The winds never ripped us from the ground or sent us spiraling into the air. We never suffered any harm, and I never felt we were in any danger. I merely held a profound respect for the power behind the storms.

These dreams occurred regularly for years. The final one was different. In that one, my hairstylist (a Christian) stood with us outside in our old neighborhood.

Filled with joy and excitement, she exclaimed, "He's coming! Jesus is coming!" She pointed to what appeared to be a brilliant parade in the sky just overhead.

The usual debris that typically precedes the controlled chaos of a tornado had been transformed into what appeared to be beautiful, shimmering ice crystals, each showing off its intricacies as it glistened and danced in the sunlight.

Next came brilliantly colored floats in the rich jeweled tones of Easter. One was wrapped in a vibrant peridot with deep-blue topaz highlights. Another shone in a vivid amethyst. Yet another was covered in a brilliant citrine color highlighted with a peach morganite border, swirled around with shimmering sparkles. Heavenly beings sat on the floats, which were breathtakingly beautiful. We stood there, gazing in awe as the sight passed above us and consumed the sky.

> **We waited expectantly for someone to take the stage, but no one did.**

Immediately following the heavenly parade, we found ourselves at the end of my street. A stage stood in the front of my yard. A traffic signal overhead had a green light and a red light, but no yellow light. We waited expectantly for someone to take the stage, but no one did.

The Matthew 14 Connection

I believe these dreams correspond with a story in Matthew 14:22–33:

Immediately after this, Jesus insisted that his disciples get back into the boat and cross to the other side of the lake while he sent the people home. After sending them home, he went up into the hills by himself to pray. Night fell while he was there alone.

Meanwhile, the disciples were in trouble far away from land, for a strong wind had risen, and they were fighting heavy waves. About three o'clock in the morning Jesus came toward them, walking on the water. When the disciples saw him walking on the water, they were terrified. In their fear, they cried out, "It's a ghost!"

But Jesus spoke to them at once. "Don't be afraid," he said. "Take courage. I am here!"

Then Peter called to him, "Lord, if it's really you, tell me to come to you, walking on the water."

"Yes, come," Jesus said.

So Peter went over the side of the boat and walked on the water toward Jesus. But when he saw the strong wind and the waves, he was terrified and began to sink. "Save me, Lord!" he shouted.

Jesus immediately reached out and grabbed him. "You have so little faith," Jesus said. "Why did you doubt me?"

When they climbed back into the boat, the wind stopped. Then the disciples worshiped him. "You really are the Son of God!" they exclaimed.

Storms of Life

If there's one thing we can count on, it's that we will constantly face storms. During those times, we can keep our heads above water with our eyes transfixed on Jesus. Or we can be overwhelmed by the storm, unable to discern the wind from the waves and the rain and—like Peter—sink into the abyss.

> We cannot control our circumstances, but we can control our focus.

I love the part of the story where Peter found himself sinking, and all he had to do was reach up to Jesus and ask for help, and Jesus was there for him.

God used my dreams to make Scripture meaningful to me and to make a deep impression on my heart so I would recognize His voice.

In Matthew 14:29, Jesus told Peter, "Come." With his eyes focused on Jesus, he stepped out of the boat he had been clinging to as a source of safety and protection. As he gazed into the eyes of Jesus, Peter walked on water in the midst of a storm without fear. The disciples believed they had seen a ghost, but Peter put his trust in Jesus to protect him from the storm. His goal was not to get to the shore; his goal was to move closer to Jesus.

This is what we all need to do. When we lock eyes with Jesus, everything on the periphery (our friends, the wind and waves of life's storms, and our earthly sources of security) will grow dim. We cannot control our circumstances, but we can control our focus. He encourages us to look into His eyes, let go of whatever we're clinging to, and reach out to Him, because He wants to rescue us.

When God led me to Matthew 14, I realized the purpose of my recurring dreams about storms. He used them to speak obedience, faith, and purpose into my life so I would recognize His voice. I am blessed to know that even when I'm sleeping, God keeps His hand on me.

Chapter 6
Waiting on God

Sometimes we need to see an image-bearer of our Creator in action. A person steeped in authenticity and living out their belief in God as a faithful disciple by walking in kindness, treating others with gentleness and respect, and lifting others' spirits by demonstrating the love Jesus showed through His sacrifice on the cross. For me, that man was Ron.

A middle-aged man who owned a construction company, Ron regularly stopped at the coffee shop where I worked between the ages of twenty and twenty-seven. He often brought his crew in for lunch, and he came in on weekends with his family. He generously paid for his crew's meals and always left a good tip for his waitress. Although he employed some "interesting" characters, he treated them with compassion and respect. They in turn respected him.

Like Jesus, Ron displayed love for some who might seem unlovable.

His acts of kindness went beyond those of a typical patron. He once gave me a ceramic cat perched on its hind legs, front legs extended forward and playfully grasping a ball of yarn. I treasured that simple, unexpected gift. One time for my birthday, he blessed me with a black Scottish terrier cookie jar filled to the top—not with cookies but dollar bills.

Some might have considered this suspicious behavior, but I knew the story behind the actions. He was living out the Great Commission by loving people to Christ. His tangible blessings set him apart. Knowing he was a Christian, I had a deep respect for him, even though I didn't have a personal relationship with Jesus at the time.

Ron was a highlight of my seven years as a waitress and a primary reason I loved that job. I met all kinds of people and came to know some of the patrons quite well. A few of them, like Ron, left lasting impressions. I am confident there are no chance meetings. I believe God perfectly orchestrates every encounter for His perfect purpose.

A Battered Life

At fourteen, I went to live with my mother. During the second semester of ninth grade I became rebellious. I skipped school every afternoon to hang out with friends, smoke marijuana, and drink alcohol. By the time my mother found out, I had flunked out of all my afternoon classes.

The following summer, I ran away from home to live with my boyfriend at his parents' house on my grandmother's reservation. By the time my father tracked me down, I had tasted freedom, and there was no way I was going to live at home again. I was sexually active, which I believed made me an adult.

> My unsophisticated, blighted juvenile mind was closed off to living life any other way.

Yet I continued behaving like a juvenile delinquent. I was completely detached from school, family, and God. My unsophisticated, blighted juvenile mind was closed off to living life any other way.

Not surprisingly, I became pregnant at sixteen. My mother begrudgingly agreed to sign the parental consent form for underage marriage. Without telling my father, we went to the neighboring state of Idaho for the ceremony. On December 10, wearing blue-and-white engineer overalls and a white satin jacket, I married my boyfriend at a place called The Hitching Post.

There were no flowers, no bridesmaids, no rings. No wedding dress or veil, and no father giving me away. I know it broke my parents' hearts, as well as God's. But I was experiencing the consequences of my choices.

To no one's surprise, the marriage was disastrous. It was riddled with alcohol, anger, and infidelity. The devil must have let out raucous laughter, celebrating his victory through my failure. My daughter suffered the collateral damage of the devastation and brokenness orchestrated by Satan.

Somehow, the marriage lasted five years. I was afraid to leave. I had no education, job skills, money, driver's license, or a vehicle. I lacked self-confidence and self-esteem and possessed no tools to navigate life. I had squandered my God-given gifts of intelligence and leadership skills. To the world I was nothing more than another teen pregnancy statistic.

I had bad hair and couldn't cook. My home was always a mess, reflecting my inner turmoil. I smoked like a chimney. A hideous role model for my child, I felt like a terrible mother and a prisoner in my own home.

When the uranium mine where my husband worked closed down, he collected unemployment for a while, but it ran out, leaving us broke.

Bad to Worse

Unable to continue living independently, we moved into my mother's two-bedroom apartment in Spokane. An old friend from school worked at a local coffee shop, and she encouraged me to apply to work with her. I lied about my experience and got hired on the spot. Even though I worked the graveyard shift, I loved my job. At the age of twenty, for the first time in my life, I was earning money.

One Friday night a couple of weeks after I started working, my husband declared he wanted to go out with his friends and gave me the responsibility of finding a babysitter. In that moment I found my voice. My eyes flashing in anger, I told him to find his own sitter.

Feeling tired and defeated, I told my mother I wanted out of my marriage. She agreed to let me stay with her temporarily. As much as it hurt to separate, I kicked my husband out.

He took our daughter and left to go live with his parents. As he pulled away in his 1978 Ford pickup, my little girl standing in the front passenger seat, my heart broke. Like my mother did to me, I was abandoning my daughter while hoping for a better life. I knew I couldn't stay in the marriage, but I also knew I was not equipped to be a good parent by myself.

> As he pulled away in his 1978 Ford pickup, my little girl standing in the front passenger seat, my heart broke.

I met my second husband while working as a waitress. Several years later, that marriage was also in trouble.

My daughter came to live with us when she was in the second grade. After two years apart, parenting was unfamiliar for both of us, as well as my husband, who had unrealistic expectations for a child.

We failed miserably.

By the time she reached puberty, her childhood emotional trauma, budding hormones, and numerous misunderstandings all blew up. She began acting out in rebellion. One day after school she went to a friend's house and refused to come home.

Another time, while we were at work, she stole my husband's car for the day. Stating that she hated us, she moved in with her father, which broke my heart yet again.

Numb with Grief

On the phone with my sister, I tearfully shared my hopelessness and grief over losing my daughter. She had moved to Michigan and shortly after became a born-again Christian. She asked if she could pray for me. Having nothing to lose, I conceded.

Calls with my sister became a regular occurrence. As she prayed aloud for me, asking God to heal my broken relationship with my daughter, I listened eagerly. Her prayers were genuine, heartfelt, and applicable, not the memorized, mechanical-sounding prayers I had once uttered. They touched my heart.

During one of those phone conversations, my sister led me to profess faith in Jesus as my Lord and Savior. Having come to the end of myself, I surrendered my will to His.

A year later, my mother and I traveled to Michigan to visit my sister over Mother's Day weekend. While we were there, my sister invited me to attend her Bible study. Though I had recited the sinner's prayer, confessed my sins, and asked Jesus into my life, I wasn't sure how to live out my new faith. My heart was open to anything God might have to offer me, so I agreed to accompany her to that Bible study while my mother stayed with my sister's children.

When we arrived at the host's home, God met me there in a way I had never experienced before.

One woman in the group had gotten into a fight with her daughter that morning. She asked for prayer and healing. Many of the women placed their hands on Mary's head and shoulders, while others reached toward her with their hands outstretched as an act of blessing. Everyone prayed. I had never participated in anything like this. But with complete submission to God and a willing heart, I bowed my head and silently joined the group.

I felt a hand on my head and the group leader began praying aloud for me. In a profound encounter with the Holy Spirit, I experienced a life-changing moment. A rush of warmth poured over me. I sobbed uncontrollably, my entire body trembling.

As quickly as this rush of overwhelming emotion came over me, it was gone. In its place came a peace like I had never felt. I recognized it as the perfect peace of Christ that surpasses all understanding.

Transformed by the Spirit

I left that meeting transformed—filled with the Holy Spirit. That day marked a major step forward in my walk with God. I fully embraced His forgiveness and willingly accepted His gift of grace. I had a deeper knowledge of what submitting to Him meant and a newfound appreciation for my identity as a child of the King. I was redeemed. Hallelujah!

Before this amazing transformation, I went to parties every weekend and drank to the point of vomiting on a regular basis. I looked for attention outside my marriage. Profanity littered every sentence that came out of my mouth. I abandoned my daughter when she was five years old. I was a selfish, self-loathing mess.

I returned home from Michigan a changed person. I was so different my husband suspected I had joined a cult. He detested my new habit of carrying my Bible everywhere. He gradually withdrew from me, and after eight months, he told me he wanted a divorce. I begged him to reconsider. He wouldn't budge. When he filed for divorce a couple of months later, I moved into my own apartment.

My husband blamed the divorce on my relationship with the Lord. But our marriage was tarnished from indiscretion even before we married. I don't believe my husband had fully recovered from the heartbreak of my previous infidelity.

I sat in my one-bedroom apartment alone since my daughter had gone to live with her father months earlier. As much as I loved the Lord, I longed for human companionship. I wasn't emotionally equipped to deal with profound solitude. I felt lonely, rejected, and abandoned.

Instead of seeking comfort in the Lord, I tried to fill this painful void through a new relationship with a man I knew from work, even before my divorce was finalized.

Submitting to God

Through the women in my Bible study group, God told me I had to speak to my estranged husband about restoring our relationship. I felt like Abraham when God ordered him to sacrifice Isaac. I didn't want to do it, but I knew I had to obey. And if the man who'd filed for divorce from me two months earlier wanted to restore the marriage, I knew I would have to say goodbye to my new love.

Though my heart was breaking, I met with him and told him if there was any chance he wanted to restore the marriage, I was willing to try. He had no interest in reconciliation. He had moved on to a new relationship and told me to go on with my life.

What a relief! Just as God provided a way out once Abraham had proven his faith, He blessed my heart of obedience. Even though getting involved in a romantic relationship while I was still legally married was a sin.

> Just as God provided a way out once Abraham had proven his faith, he blessed my heart of obedience.

During that time of immense pain and brokenness, I recognized that in my weakness, just like Abraham, I had taken matters into my own hands. God blessed Abraham, even though he sinned, and the Lord blessed me even in my sin. I had reached out for human companionship instead of trusting in the Lord, and God was merciful.

He is all I need. And because of His grace, I found blessings. Years after my waitressing days ended, I visited my friend Ron from the restaurant. I knew he had been praying for me, and I wanted him to know his prayers had finally been answered. The kindness and compassion he'd demonstrated as a Christian were a powerful part of my journey to Christ. He never preached to me, but his quiet faith spoke volumes about what it means to be a Christian. Ron provided living evidence that God had a hand on me all those years earlier as a waitress in a coffee shop, before I even knew that I was waiting on God.

Miracles in Ethiopia

While I was working in Spokane as a paramedic, a flier appeared on the bulletin board with information about a physician assistant satellite training program from the University of Washington. They were holding an informational meeting for those interested in pursuing a PA career.

The seed of interest in a higher plane of medical training had been planted back in 1992, almost immediately after I received my paramedic certification. My father, who worked as a public health educator, said to me, "Congratulations! Now you can work on becoming a PA."

This was something I really wanted to do. I'd questioned whether I would be good enough to reach that level and doubted it would ever become a reality. It would require taking night classes, volunteering in the community, shadowing other PAs, and traveling for training so I could be the best candidate possible. But when the bulletin board flier caught my eye that day, I knew it had been posted especially for me.

At the informational meeting, I discovered I needed to take classes in anatomy, physiology, biology, and English before I could apply to the university's PA program. That would be challenging, especially with a two-year-old at home! But I stepped out in faith, believing I could do it if it was God's will

> With childlike faith, I prayed this simple prayer: **God, I want to be a physician assistant**.

for my life. With childlike faith, I prayed this simple prayer: God, I want to be a physician assistant. If this is not in Your will for me, please close the door. But if You close the door, please slam it shut so I will know You mean it. Because I want this so much, I will not give up easily.

Navigating Registration

I somehow managed to navigate the college registration thing and sign up for my first prerequisite class. That alone was a huge accomplishment, having dropped out of school in the ninth grade.

Before that point I'd been an A student, a promising athlete, and a student leader. I'd won my school spelling bee, represented my community at the state science fair, and secured first- and second-place finishes in district speech competitions in the Original Oratory category. I had so much going for me. But it wasn't enough to subdue the emptiness and ache deep inside my soul. It didn't quench my overwhelming desire to feel loved and accepted. So I turned to alcohol. And flew to Spokane to live with my mother.

Some kids who experiment with drugs and alcohol at an early age end up in prison, foster homes, psychiatric wards, or a cemetery. God's grace protected me from those fates.

Despite my mistakes, God loved me so much that He sent His one and only Son to die for me. He allows me to choose my will over His, and sometimes I haven't trusted Him. But God remains faithful even when I'm not.

Even so, my choices impact others. And there are always consequences for sin.

Seeking Acceptance

God allows us to reap the consequences of the havoc we sow. Sometimes we experience collateral damage from the sins of our parents, and God uses it to speak lessons into their lives. Sometimes God disciplines us for our own sins so we will grow from the experience. My situation was a little of both.

I came from brokenness, and that created brokenness for my daughter. But a loving God changed my story. His Word is filled with promises of restoration, healing, and victory over all kinds of evil. Deuteronomy 31:8 says He will never leave me or forsake me. Romans 8:28 says He will work everything for good for me, because He has called me according to His purpose.

I worked nights, which meant being away from home between six o'clock in the evening and six in the morning. The night dispatcher had been kind to me, so I considered introducing him to a single friend of my cousin. When I suddenly found myself on the verge of being single myself, I invited him to dinner at my apartment instead.

Brad and I spent a lot of time together that summer. Just two months after our first date, he proposed. Another two months later, we were married. We have been married for nearly three decades now, and I love him more today than ever. He supports me in everything I do and has been my biggest champion since day one.

Starting Classes

My second husband had pushed me to get my GED, which made me eligible to attend paramedic school. My experience as a paramedic opened the door for college prerequisite classes for PA school.

I started with an introduction to biology. In that class I met a beautiful Christian woman from Ethiopia named Aster. She had a heart full of joy and a contagious smile. Aster was the first person I'd ever known who came from another country.

During our time together in night school, we became fast friends. We studied together and rode to campus together. I vowed that if I ever had the opportunity to travel to Ethiopia, I would go. Little did I know at the time

> **Aster was the first person I'd ever known who came from another country.**

what God had planned for me. As Jeremiah 29:11 says, "'I know the plans I have for you,' says the Lord. 'They are plans for good and not for disaster, to give you a future and a hope.'"

Eighteen years after those first college classes, the opportunity to visit Ethiopia arose when my church cosponsored a medical mission trip to this African nation and a friend asked if I wanted to go. I had already used some of my vacation time for the year, so I didn't have enough left, which meant I'd have to take time off without pay. But I didn't want to say no without consulting God. I told my friend I would pray about it.

Brad and I had been saving up to purchase some land in Hawaii to build a retirement home, so we had some extra money. I asked God, If this is Your will for me, please let me know. Within twenty minutes, God led me to a passage from Luke 12:16–21, where Jesus told His disciples this story:

> A rich man had a fertile farm that produced fine crops. He said to himself, "What should I do? I don't have room for all my crops." Then he said, "I know! I'll tear down my barns and build bigger ones. Then I'll have room enough to store all my wheat and other goods. And I'll sit back and say to myself, 'My friend, you have enough stored for years to come. Now take it easy! Eat, drink, and be merry!'"
> But God said to him, "You fool! You will die this very night. Then who will get everything you worked for?"
> Yes, a person is a fool to store up earthly wealth but not have a rich relationship with God.

Certain this was my answer, I shared that Scripture with my husband. "Our plans to purchase a small plot in Hawaii are like building barns. I'm being called to spend money on a medical mission trip to Ethiopia to store up treasures in heaven." Brad faithfully agreed.

God sealed the deal with a song. As I drove to meet a friend for lunch, the song "Oceans" came on the radio, which begins with the lyricist talking about God calling him to walk on the water. I immediately thought of the story from Matthew 14 where Peter walked on water.

I knew without a doubt I was supposed to go to Ethiopia. My heart was full of excitement.

God revealed His will to me in a personal way—a way I would understand. He used a friendship established eighteen years earlier to plant a seed in my heart so that when He called me, I would listen.

Trusting in God

In Ethiopia, we went to a place called the Blood Village. Human sacrifice was still practiced there, and the town was basically ruled by a witch doctor. Many of the people practiced animism, which teaches that objects, places, and creatures all possess a spirit. Others were Muslims, and some belonged to the Ethiopian Orthodox church.

Only one evangelical Christian man there recognized the power of the cross. A church planter, things weren't going in his favor. Days before we arrived, he had been imprisoned and all of his belongings stolen. That probably would've been enough for me to lose faith. But God had other plans for that man and that community.

When we arrived, the air was heavy with humidity and dust. A few of us felt ill, and the leader encouraged us to pray because we were going into spiritual battle with the enemy. He prayed all night for healing and safety for the team.

I prayed but soon fell asleep, just like the apostles did when Jesus asked them to pray for Him. When I awoke, my illness was gone. A miraculous answer to prayer. Hallelujah!

Working Miracles

While the townspeople may have been a bit curious about us foreigners, they did not welcome us with open arms.

In spite of our cool reception, we got right to work setting up our free medical clinic. People came in droves. While many allowed us to pray for them, others politely declined.

> Human sacrifice was still practiced there, and the town was basically ruled by a witch doctor.

As we sat in a darkened room with floors made of earth and walls of dried mud, one mother and her son of around fourteen approached us. Through the aid of our interpreter, she told us he'd been having seizures and he couldn't speak a word. They had walked a long distance seeking treatment.

In all my years of caring for patients, this was a first for me. I knew I had nothing to offer this desperate mother for her son's seizures, and I was not prepared to address his inability to express himself verbally. So I gave him what I had. I laid my hands on him and prayed for God to heal him.

"Lord, You are the Great Physician and You can heal this boy. I ask You to give him his voice so he can use it to worship You, giving You all the glory."

I still felt helplessness, but then I remembered I wasn't there to practice medicine but to share Christ's love. By praying for this boy and his mother, I did what I was called there to do. I envisioned myself stepping out of the boat onto the water. I lifted my eyes off the waves in front of me and looked into the eyes of Jesus. Then I moved on to the next patient.

Twenty minutes later, our team leader entered the area, carrying a camera. With a sense of excitement he asked, "Who saw the boy who couldn't speak?"

"I did," I responded.

"Then you want to see this," he said.

The boy and his mother walked in. His hands raised to the heavens in praise, he exclaimed with his own voice, "Iyesus getanew!" (Jesus is Lord). I broke out sobbing.

Blessed Participation

God helped me see past the lies and imperfections of my human condition and allowed me to participate in a miracle firsthand. Not only did He have a hand on this boy and his mother, He also had a hand on me.

> His hands raised to the heavens in praise, he exclaimed with his own voice, "Iyesus getanew!" (Jesus is Lord).

Healing miracles exist here in America as well, but we are often too busy to see them. We don't allow ourselves to move beyond our comfort zones and don't always listen to God's voice guiding us to where He wants us to go on His behalf. My experience in Ethiopia taught me to ask expectantly for God to perform miracles.

In 1992, I had lunch with three respected Christian leaders: a cardiologist, the CEO of a nonprofit African church-planting ministry, and an Ethiopian man who oversees church plants in the Horn of Africa. The CEO, Erik, was also the group leader of our medical mission trip. Our trip happened because of a vision that the cardiologist, Jared, shared with Erik. Garedew, who lives in Ethiopia and regularly visits the Pacific Northwest, took us to the Blood Village. He oversaw everything we did on our medical mission.

As I shared a meal with three men I never would have met if not for God's intervention in my life, I smiled at this tangible evidence of a powerful God strategically aligning my steps and using everything to accomplish His will. These men, like my friend Aster, are humble servants of the King. They are blessings in my life and evidence of God's amazing love for this world.

Chapter 8

Opening More Doors

After several years of ambulance duty, I wanted more "tools for my tool-box." This longing had a spiritual connection. Psalm 37:4 says, "Take delight in the Lord, and he will give you your heart's desires." God knew my heart's desires. I'd had dreams of becoming a doctor since the eighth grade.

Tough Road Ahead

A Native American woman visited my aunt's workplace and dropped off some fliers about a PA program in Southern California. She shared the information with me. I called and learned the woman was recruiting Native students to visit the University of Southern California to attend the Health Careers Opportunity Program to develop their application skills. The final goal: acceptance to a PA program.

I told her I had no intention of applying to a school in California. She flew me to Los Angeles anyway, put me up in a hotel, and trained me, equipping me with the tools I would need to become the strongest possible applicant. I put my heart and soul into the process and ended up wanting it more than anything. Gaining acceptance into that program became my god, and I was willing to be whoever I thought they wanted me to be to achieve that goal.

The first year I applied I was rejected. While some might think, It wasn't your time, I felt like an absolute failure. I remembered the prayer I prayed before applying to PA school, asking God to open the door if this was His will for my life and if it weren't, to slam it shut. I might have been able to make things happen by begging, pleading, pushing, or getting obnoxious, but I didn't want to be that person. God had closed the door. But He didn't slam it.

The second year of applications came and went with no phone call of acceptance. I was disappointed and saddened, but we didn't have the $60,000 the program would cost anyway.

During my prayer time, I heard this message: If you don't get in after three tries, it probably isn't a good fit. I took that as a sign from God. I decided

> **When I finally let go of a control I never really possessed, God came through for me in a bigger way than I ever hoped or imagined.**

I would apply one last time the following year. If I wasn't accepted, I would go to nursing school, which was more affordable anyway.

One More Try

I spent the next year doing everything in my power to make myself a stronger applicant. Then I stopped trying and mentally prepared myself for the idea that I would likely end up going to nursing school instead. I applied for scholarships, even though I didn't expect to need them.

When I finally let go of a control I never really possessed, God came through for me in a bigger way than I ever hoped or imagined.

The third and final time I applied to the program, I received the phone call! I was offered two nationally awarded full-ride scholarships, both coveted and sought after. Each of these scholarships had between 1,200 and 1,800 contenders, with only about 10 percent of applicants receiving the award. Receiving one would have been a blessing! But both was truly an act of God.

Each scholarship covered all educational fees, including tuition, books, and equipment plus a monthly stipend that almost equaled my salary as a paramedic. My biggest challenge was to select the right one for me.

Both scholarships required a minimum of two years of service in a medically underserved area, based on certain health-industry criteria. I chose the one that would allow me to remain in eastern Washington rather than possibly having to relocate to a faraway state.

For two years my commute took me away from home four days during the week. Still, the opportunity to complete PA schooling without incurring a mountain of debt was an answer to prayer that far exceeded all my hopes and expectations. During my training I experienced no financial stress or educational burdens.

Chapter 9

Return to Ethiopia

Three years after my first visit to Ethiopia, I had the opportunity to travel there again on a second medical mission trip. Excitement surged in my spirit and my heart leapt for joy.

But as the time drew closer, I felt hesitant, which made me question whether going back to Ethiopia was indeed God's will for me. Either way, I knew if I obeyed God, I would be blessed.

When we are walking with the Lord, we can count on Satan's attempts to thwart God's plans, so we must remain vigilant. I was living out my faith, believing a blessing would follow, but it was not the blessing that motivated me ... it was a desire to be obedient to the Lord.

The devil raised doubts, fears, and uncertainties in my mind. One issue was the cost: around $3,000, plus the sacrifice of two weeks of vacation time. Not to mention the risk and discomfort associated with travel.

In addition, my fear of spiders and other creepy crawlies always felt more robust in warmer climates. I envisioned the sky raining spiders down on me, even though that hadn't happened when I went to Ethiopia before.

> I was living out my faith, believing a blessing would follow, but it was not the blessing that motivated me.

I also faced the fear of contracting a fatal illness, the potential risk of dying in a plane crash, and the possibility of a terrorist attack in a post-9/11 world.

Though I felt a strong reluctance to go, God clearly showed me I was created to do this. And so I went.

Great Rewards

The rewards of going on this trip made such a deep impression on me, I wrote about it in my journal. Here is an excerpt:

Yesterday I awoke in Paradise—Paradise Lodge, that is—in a place called Arba Minch, which means "40 Springs." It was a beautiful summer day, perfect for our long drive to Addis Ababa.

Over the past fourteen days, our team has spent nearly every moment together, eager to learn about one another, side by side, as we served the Lord. After a two-hour drive to Sodo, we separated into two teams.

Before we went our separate ways, Erik prayed for a good day of travel and easy goodbyes. I was thankful for that, because I struggle with goodbyes.

We took turns embracing our newfound brothers and sisters in Christ. We blessed one another, realizing that we might not cross paths again this side of paradise. But knowing we would meet again in heaven lessened the burden of parting. How could it be so difficult to say goodbye to someone I only met two weeks ago? During this brief time, we experienced phenomenal spiritual treasures together, creating an immeasurable bond. I believe each one of us walked away a richer person. And with every farewell, a piece of my heart went with them.

> I encountered God in Ethiopia through the hearts of those whose lives were briefly intertwined with mine.

As I process the events of the past week, I remain in awe of the works God created us to walk in and the miracles He allowed us to be a part of. I am reminded of the internal strife I encountered the day before the trip—my tearful reluctance battling my desire to be obedient. Obedience won.

As I embraced my Ethiopian brothers and sisters one last time, I thought, Here is my reward.

I have come away a better person because I chose obedience. I encountered God in Ethiopia through the hearts of those whose lives were briefly intertwined with mine. My trust and faith were strengthened, and the works I was called to walk through no longer seem overwhelming.

I knew as I entered the journey He would bless my obedience, but I had no way of predicting the amount of spiritual riches I would receive as a result. I am abundantly overwhelmed by God's loving embrace.

Faith and Deeds

In reflecting on this trip, several passages from the book of James came to mind:

- James 1:2–4: "Dear brothers and sisters, when troubles of any kind come your way, consider it an opportunity for great joy. For you know that when your faith is tested, your endurance has a chance to grow. So let it grow, for when your endurance is fully developed, you will be perfect and complete, needing nothing."

This Scripture spoke to my heart as I returned from Ethiopia, knowing the blessing I received through obedience. I faced trials. I faced my fears. I encountered a couple of fist-sized spiders and lived through it. Although I can still see the spiders in my head, I came through with so much more.

- James 1:12: "God blesses those who patiently endure testing and temptation. Afterward they will receive the crown of life that God has promised to those who love Him."

- James 1:22–25: "Don't just listen to God's word. You must do what it says. Otherwise, you are only fooling yourselves. For if you listen to the word and don't obey, it is like glancing at your face in a mirror. You see yourself, walk away, and forget what you look like. But if you look carefully into the perfect law that sets you free, and if you do what it says and don't forget what you heard, then God will bless you for doing it."

- James 2:14–17: "What good is it, dear brothers and sisters, if you say you have faith but don't show it by your actions? Can that kind of faith save anyone? Suppose you see a brother or sister who has no food or clothing, and you say, 'Good-bye and have a good day; stay warm and eat well'—but then you don't give that person any food or clothing. What good does that do? So you see, faith by itself isn't enough. Unless it produces good deeds, it is dead and useless."

Walking through Trials

When God called me back to Ethiopia, He equipped me to walk victoriously through the deeds he wanted me to accomplish and He accompanied me on the journey. He blesses me today by reminding me that through my obedience and trust in Him I have stored up treasures in heaven.

These truths also blessed me after I returned from Ethiopia. Back home, I faced uncertainties entering the latter stages of life. I encountered fragility in an uncomfortably personal way. I wanted to escape my circumstances, but I knew God had allowed them for His purpose.

A test of faith came when I developed a potentially serious case of shingles.

> **From within this darkness, I heard God's familiar, still small voice reminding me to get into His Word.**

I experienced the loss of my patellar reflex—what many people recognize as the knee-jerk reaction. Being unable to move properly would threaten my livelihood in the medical field. Overwhelming fear crept over me and consumed my thoughts. I struggled to overcome my fear, but ever-present pain left me exhausted.

From within this darkness, I heard God's familiar, still small voice reminding me to get into His Word. In obedience, I reached out to Him. Recognizing the weakness of my mortal condition, I went back to writing about how God had a hand on me.

In that moment, the Lord revealed Himself again. He reminded me He was with me. He had allowed the singles outbreak to occur and He would bring me through it. I didn't need to walk in fear.

The devil "prowls around like a roaring lion, looking for someone to devour" (1 Pet. 5:8). You'd think I would have realized the truth of this because of my second trip to Ethiopia. But no matter how many times you've seen God come through for you in the past, the enemy still tries to depress, confuse, and upset you. Whenever this happens, I turn to the apostle's exhortation in verse 9: "Stand firm against him, and be strong in your faith."

Muscles gain strength with exercise. Exercising our faith isn't easy, but it will bring victory.

Chapter 10

The Marathon

In 2003, just before I turned forty, a charity fundraising/endurance sports training program sparked my interest. Only a year prior, I wouldn't have imagined myself getting off my perfectly good sofa to run a mile, much less the 26.2 miles it takes to complete a full marathon. But this one was in Hawaii, where my husband and I had contemplated one day retiring. If I could raise $3,000 and train three to five times a week, I could join thousands of others to help find a cure for cancer by running the Honolulu Marathon that December.

I was never a distance runner, not even when I ran track in the seventh and eighth grades. At thirty-nine I couldn't run a block without gasping for air and surrendering to exhaustion. What was I thinking, signing up to run 26.2 miles?

As ugly as training felt in the beginning, never once did I consider it impossible. Nor did I doubt that I could raise the money to help find a cure for cancer. I was motivated! So out my front door I went, wearing the only tennis shoes I owned.

I went through a lot of huffing and puffing preparing for my first goal: running a couple of miles in preparation for the program's first group run of three miles.

A Caring Coach

My coach and my mentor started with several information sessions to help me learn about running gear and stretching. They also reviewed proper nutrition and hydration for endurance events. I embraced their instructions with enthusiasm and vigor.

Since our goal was to raise money for research to help cure cancer, we were each assigned an "honored patient": a person going through cancer treatment. When we struggled with the distance of training runs or didn't feel like putting in the miles, we could think of our patients for encouragement and inspiration to keep going. It worked.

My coach was one of the most humble people I have ever met. He taught me to love running. He refers to me as his success story, knowing my self-proclaimed couch-potato status before we met. He once told me his goal as a coach was to get people like me to love running so much it would become a life sport for them.

Some twenty years after my first marathon, I still enjoy running. I love it so much that I always have a pair of running shoes with me so I can run wherever I go. I've planned trips around races I signed up for.

Running is like my relationship with Jesus: it has made my life better and requires discipline in order to excel. And with both, my only regret is that I didn't start sooner.

The Honolulu Marathon was the first of many endurance events for me. I don't run fast or pretty, but I have seen some pretty amazing places I never would have visited otherwise.

Fooled by the Devil

Life has a way of taking unexpected turns.

After completing my first marathon, I signed up for another event with that same endurance training program. During the post-race celebration, I decided a little drink couldn't hurt. So after eight years of living alcohol-free,

> Running is like my relationship with Jesus: it has made my life better and requires discipline in order to excel.

I had a glass of wine. I was a Christian, so I wasn't at risk of falling into my old ways. Right?

That was mistake number one: not realizing that as a Christian I was a prime target for the enemy. If he could trip me up and drag me down, how many others would go down with me?

Not only did the devil fool me into believing I was untouchable, I was blinded by the world. God allowed the enemy to lure me into darkness. Sadly, I went willingly. I literally ran there.

In a short period of time, I went from having a single glass of wine to drinking an entire bottle by myself. I bought into the lie that I was in control.

But God revealed the truth to me as I sat in church one Sunday and the pastor said, "If there is something keeping you from growing closer to the Lord, He wants you to give it up."

I heard the message as clear as a bell … not audibly but deep down in my heart. Alcohol was hindering my spiritual growth. Three days later, I told a friend about my experience.

"You don't have to give up alcohol completely," she said.

That didn't sit right with me. I knew what God had said. Needing a second opinion, I told my husband, who had sat next to me that Sunday. Brad's initial response was the same: he told me he didn't think I had to quit completely.

But the message I heard from God was that I needed to completely abstain if I wanted to be obedient, because alcohol was keeping me from growing closer to Him. The Lord knows I'm the kind of person who can't stop at one drink. I will drink until I can't see straight, then get in my car and drive home, endangering my life and others.

God was giving me a choice: follow Him or remain on the path to destruction. When I told my husband again, this time he agreed. We quit drinking as quickly as we had started.

Saving Myself

God knew long before I was born how He would use the circumstances of my life for His glory. How He would use the brokenness the enemy meant for harm and turn it into good. Even how He would use my understanding of alcoholism to speak His truth into the lives of the people He placed in my path.

All for His glory!

We all have our own burdens. Mine was alcohol. Other people worship different things, like their phones, wealth, pride, prestige, sex, youth, social media, self, career, power...the list goes on. If we listen, we will hear God speak to us regarding our idols. He wants to be the only God in our lives; there is no room for imposters.

So I gave up alcohol, but I kept running. That led to cycling, and my running and cycling progressed to triathlons. Through triathlon competitions God placed several people in my life.

> ## He has taken my painful circumstances and turned them into a testimony.

I have been blessed by many amazing moments, and when I think of where I started, it is almost unbelievable. I came from brokenness and abandonment, and today my life is rich and full. I sit in awe of how richly God has blessed my life. He has taken my painful circumstances and turned them into a testimony.

Because of running, I especially relate to the athletically related musings of the apostle Paul: "I press on to reach the end of the race and receive the heavenly prize for which God, through Christ Jesus, is calling us" (Phil. 3:14) and "I have fought the good fight, I have finished the race, and I have remained faithful" (2 Tim. 4:7). I am so glad God guided me back to the right path and that—despite a short fall—I have remained faithful.

Chapter 11
Test of Endurance

It's good to be active and maintain our health. But it's hard to train for a 70.3-mile Half Ironman (1.2-mile swim, 56-mile bike ride, and 13.1-mile run) or a 140.6-mile Ironman triathlon without—at least on some level—making it your god. Either the journey becomes an idol or we lapse into worship of self.

I did my first full Ironman for myself and my own glory. While my accomplishments may be inspirational to some, and I can use them as an avenue to encourage others, crossing that finish line was all about me.

Despite my shortcomings, God placed some of my dearest friends in my path, and He has been glorified through those relationships. One friend who comes to mind is my coach, Scott. He trained me for my first sprint triathlon. This race challenged me to persevere through self-doubt.

About a fourth of the way into the 400-meter swim, I began struggling, thinking I wasn't going to make it. I flipped over and backstroked the rest of the way. Regardless of my lack of skill and speed, Scott encouraged me to keep moving forward.

I moved up in distance after that, and with only one triathlon under my belt, I fearlessly started training for a 70.3-mile race. It took me nearly the full allotted time to complete the course. (I got lost on the swim and missed the first turn, swimming probably one hundred yards more than required.) But I made it to the finish line in time to earn a medal.

Training for these long-distance events means spending several hours in the pool, on the bike, and running. I have enjoyed being in the company of like-minded people, building relationships, and developing camaraderie as we sort of adopt one another as family. God has used those relationships to accomplish His will, and they have been a blessing to me.

Scott's time on earth was cut short for those of us left behind. At age thirty-eight, while we were at church one Sunday evening with his wife, the pastor invited people to the front, welcoming anyone who needed prayer or wanted to commit their life to Jesus. As Scott's wife entered into God's presence through prayer, her dear husband's heart stopped and his spirit left the earth, destined for God's presence for eternity.

At the funeral, I learned that Scott knew about Jesus long before he developed a relationship with Him. In his final year of life, Scott began experiencing serious health problems while training and he required a heart valve replacement. Christian neighbors and friends, including me, encouraged him to deepen his faith. We were blessed to witness God's glory when Scott submitted his life to the Lord.

Honoring Coach's Memory

Before Scott passed, many of us signed up to compete in a 70.3-mile race together. After losing our friend, the race served as a tribute to honor his memory.

Having lost my coach, my motivation and training suffered.

The June race day started as a complete nightmare, with temperatures in the forties. As we huddled together in our wetsuits before the swimming competition, one of my friends' lips turned blue from the cold. By comparison, the fifty-two-degree lake felt like bath water. The race officials shortened the length of the bike ride due to concerns about hypothermia, and a couple of women rode the bikes in their wetsuits.

> **Having lost my coach, my motivation and training suffered.**

This was a race Scott had been training for when he passed, so crossing the finish line would be bittersweet. It symbolized an indescribable void that was left in a journey we started together but had to finish without him.

During the run the sun came out, but I couldn't smile. Emotionally I was spent. If we hadn't decided to do this race together, I probably wouldn't have done it. But I made it through the arctic swim and the abbreviated bike ride. All that stood between me and the finish line was the 13.1-mile run.

During the run, one of my other teammates saw me walking, looking defeated. When I told her I was experiencing some GI discomfort, she offered me an anti-gas tablet from her race belt. I had only met her one other time, but her act of kindness made her an instant friend.

Deb didn't know me, but she asked if she could pray for me. In her prayer, she acknowledged our missing coach and asked God for the courage and strength to go on without him.

We crossed the finish line together, and many more since then. Today Deb is a dear friend, part of my Bible Study Fellowship group, and a beloved sister in Christ. I cheered her on for her first 140.6-mile race, and I will be there cheering as she crosses the finish line in heaven one day.

Painful Adjustment

In 2013, I signed up for another 70.3-mile Half Ironman triathlon. Soon after, I was diagnosed with degenerative disc disease of the cervical spine. With constant neck pain, I couldn't see myself ever doing another long-distance event. I'd had neck pain since 2007; I first noticed it while doing a two-hundred-mile bike ride from Seattle to Portland. I stopped for nutrition toward the end of the first day, after having ridden almost a hundred miles, and felt a sharp pain radiating from my neck between my shoulder blades. When a friend briefly massaged the area at a rest stop, I wanted to kiss her feet.

The pain gradually progressed and worsened significantly in 2011, when I did my long-distance triathlon event. Two years later, I had a couple of episodes of transient but profound weakness in both arms. The pain was so intense it dropped me to my knees, so I went to see my doctor. An MRI showed significant disc disease from the C1 to C7 vertebrae. The neurologist told me I needed surgery. However, the spine surgeon didn't agree.

I lived with the injury until 2017, when daily nagging pain brought me to the point of surrender. Tired of hurting, I saw my doctor, hoping physical therapy could offer me some relief.

Thanks to God's intervention, my doctor referred me to a physical therapist who trained with a spine specialist. She used a hard rubber wedge device to get my spine to pop. After years of daily unrelenting pain, I suddenly found relief!

After four visits, I learned to do the adjustments myself. Now, whenever I feel the pressure start to build, I use the wedge and immediately feel better. This made it possible for me to sit on a triathlon bike and complete another 70.3-mile race.

During my training for that race, though, I injured my back. I couldn't go to work for a few days. The excruciating pain prevented me from running, cycling, or swimming for about five weeks. I lost all the strength I had built up. Halfway into my training, I had to start over.

Just as my physical strength took a hit, so did my faith.

During my 70.3-mile race in Arizona, I wanted to quit early on in the swim. I knew I was capable of completing the distance, but I hadn't done an open-water swim in several months, with all my training having been done in a pool.

A reflex occurs when you put your face in cold water: you gasp and then hyperventilate uncontrollably. Sometimes that leads to panic. So I had learned to immerse myself gradually. I'd stand on the shore and put my face in the water several times, blowing bubbles until I got accustomed to the cold water.

In Arizona, there was no opportunity to get into the water to adjust until the reflex gasping subsided. As I entered the water, I gasped, then began to panic and wheeze. I felt my wetsuit compressing my throat.

To my left I saw a guy on the shore yelling to keep going. Though I didn't know him, he became my cheerleader—my

Just as my physical strength took a hit, so did my faith.

new Coach Scott. It's funny the things that come to mind when I'm in a race and my brain goes on autopilot. I recalled a swimming event a couple of years earlier.

I'd signed up with two other people to race as a team. Triathlons always start with a swim, followed by the bike race and then the run. In that competition, I had to complete a 1.2-mile swim before my teammates even had a chance to participate. I sputtered and struggled to gain composure until about halfway through the swim.

During my floundering in Arizona, that memory became an arrow in my quiver.

I glanced to my left and saw a guy doing the backstroke. I thought, At least he's moving forward. I can do that! So I rolled onto my back and did the same until I managed to catch my breath. Then I rolled back into a prone position, only to find myself desperately gasping for air again. If there'd been a kayak nearby, I would have latched on and thrown in the towel.

> Overcoming challenges in times of panic builds confidence for the next time I face similar struggles.

Since there was no kayak, I kept alternating between swimming and backstroking. About ten minutes into the swim, I managed to relax into a rhythm. At that point, I knew I could do it.

The bike ride was uneventful. But when I got to the run, I started to panic again. I would have to keep a steady pace if I wanted to make the cutoff time. I maintained my pace, and although it was one of the most mentally challenging things I have ever done, I completed the race with time still left on the clock.

As I crossed the finish line, I sobbed uncontrollably.

Endurance sports have served as a good training ground for my faith. Overcoming challenges in times of panic builds confidence for the next time I face similar struggles. Likewise, when I flounder in my faith, I can fall back on what has worked for me in the past.

Jesus is always there for us, but oftentimes we exhaust ourselves before reaching out to Him. Each time He rescues us is like another arrow in the quiver. Our faith continues to build until we finally believe that all things really are possible.

When we cross the final finish line, we'll see those who were part of our journeys standing on the sidelines cheering us in. I can imagine Jesus announcing the names of each one as they run victoriously through the Finish banner of heaven.

I find inspiration in Isaiah 49:1–4:

Listen to me, all you in distant lands!
Pay attention, you who are far away!
The Lord called me before my birth;
from within the womb he called me by name.
He made my words of judgment as sharp as a sword.
He has hidden me in the shadow of his hand.
I am like a sharp arrow in his quiver.
He said to me, "You are my servant, Israel,
and you will bring me glory."
I replied, "But my work seems so useless!
I have spent my strength for nothing and to no purpose.
Yet I leave it all in the Lord's hand;
I will trust God for my reward."

Like the prophet Isaiah, I too have had to learn to trust God for rewards that are worth more than accomplishing the impossible on a human level.

Chapter 12

Saved by Grace

I wish the change in my life could have made a stronger earthly impact on my younger brother. Dennis was five when our mother left us. I know how much that loss devastated me and can only imagine the hole it left in his heart. As adults we sometimes talked about the painful memories we shared, but I don't think he ever explored the full depth of that wound. The devil deceived him into thinking alcohol offered a way to deal with the pain and loss. He fought this battle with alcohol for much of his life.

> As adults we sometimes talked about the painful memories we shared, but I don't think he ever explored the full depth of that wound.

It hurt me to watch him act out his pain and despair. I loved him more than words can describe. He and my sister were my first playmates. We shared experiences that bound us together like no other relationship on earth ever will. While there were good times, much of Dennis's life was filled with turmoil.

Remembering the Good Times

My father, an avid motorcycle enthusiast, taught us to ride motorcycles when we were young. This was a great family bonding activity. We often retreated to the hills of Evaro, Montana, for late-afternoon rides and stream fishing. Evaro lies in the shadows of the Mission Mountains on the southern tip of the Flathead Reservation. Many call this area God's Country because the snow-capped mountains seem to touch heaven's borders. Beauty is everywhere.

Before we loaded up the bikes and returned to Missoula, my stepmother served us a delicious meal of chicken and fruit salad.

My brother developed a lifelong love of motorcycles, and he perfected his bike-handling skills as a teen when he competed in motocross racing events.

He also developed a love of music. He taught himself how to play the guitar and loved listening to Stevie Ray Vaughan.

Like many young Natives, Dennis was an excellent basketball player. He learned to play rezball, a style of basketball associated with Native Americans that features up-tempo, aggressive play, quick scoring, and aggressive defense. Dennis excelled at rezball because of his impeccable ball-handling skills.

Dennis was the first boy in our family. My mother's sisters gave birth to all girls, and my father's siblings produced six girls before another boy was born. So Dennis was the prized favorite of the grandparents for most of his life. He was a handsome guy, like my father. He enjoyed reading. His favorite outing growing up included a trip to Garden City News, a newsstand that sold periodicals and candy. My brother loved going there to get the latest edition of his favorite: *MAD* magazine.

Disaster Strikes

When I was in physician assistant school, Dennis was involved in an alcohol-related motorcycle crash. The kids who hit him were drinking and left him on the side of the road. He developed shock, likely as a result of the profound blood loss from an open femur fracture. The remaining portion of his left leg was twisted, with his foot facing in the opposite direction.

In the emergency room, an orthopedic surgeon recommended amputation because he had fractured several bones and the wounds were full of dirt. The surgeon said he could try to save the leg but suspected it would leave him with a constant battle against infection, which would result in poor healing. Our family made the decision to amputate and hope for the best.

When my brother awakened and learned part of his leg was gone, he was devastated. But that didn't stop him from riding his Harley Davidson.

His second major injury occurred when he returned home after a ride. As he turned left into his driveway, a truck struck him, fracturing his right leg. That put him in a wheelchair for a while. He struggled with unrelenting phantom limb pain, the missing part of his left leg throbbing as if it were still intact.

His doctor treated him with an anti-seizure medication often used to treat epilepsy but also used for nerve pain. It didn't help. The physician prescribed opioids, but Dennis didn't take many because he didn't want to become dependent on them.

Another crash took place shortly after he parted ways with his riding partner one night and was on his way home. It was dark, and by the time he saw the deer on the road, it was too late to avoid a collision that hurtled him and his bike off the highway. Some passersby stopped to move the deer off the road. When they did, they saw a flicker of light off the side of the road and discovered my brother.

> It was dark, and by the time he saw the deer on the road, it was too late to avoid a collision that hurtled him and his bike off the highway.

At the hospital doctors performed a procedure to relieve the intracranial pressure that had built up. If he had remained in the field, his brain would have swollen and he would have died.

The crash cost him his prized 2005 Harley Davidson Fat Boy Screaming Eagle, a riders' favorite because of its powerful engine and stocky frame. The first time I saw that bike, my brother beamed with pride as he showed it to us at my mother's house. It was a limited-edition red-and-silver model with lots of chrome—the most beautiful bike I had ever seen.

While the insurance company considered it totaled, Dennis later learned it was going to be auctioned off at a vehicle lot. Dennis went there in hopes of buying it back, circulating through the crowd to let everyone know how badly he wanted the Fat Boy. But an out-of-town buyer outbid him, leaving him heartbroken.

Fatal Injuries

Though Dennis survived, he was never the same. His head injury resulted in the display of raw emotions. He became childlike and brutally honest, yet often searched for words to express himself. He lapsed into depression.

He developed seizures, which grew worse when he drank—which he did often to combat the pain instead of taking opioids.

During this time of intense trials, God opened a door that led to tender conversations between us. We talked about the memories we shared—both painful and pleasant. The bonds built through shared laughter and tears created a deep trust that allowed me to say things to him he might not have been receptive to hearing if they came from others.

Step into Eternity

One night in the hospital, after my brother had one of his major seizures, I was the only other person there. The Holy Spirit prompted me to talk with him about his eternal security. I asked if he wanted to accept Jesus as his Savior. He said he had a desire to submit his life to the Lord.

Dennis knew about Jesus and His grace. He realized he needed it, yet he struggled because he saw himself as unworthy. He thought he was too bad to receive forgiveness.

We are all too bad to be forgiven. That's what makes salvation such an amazing gift. It's free and something we don't deserve. But through Jesus's amazing grace and profoundly fierce, immeasurable love for us, He sacrificed His life for our sin and imperfection. An all-knowing, all-powerful, loving God knew long before we were ever born every sin we would ever commit. And still, He created a bridge for us so we wouldn't have to live in separation from Him.

Jesus paid in full a debt we could never begin to pay. As Ephesians 2:9 puts it, "Salvation is not a reward for the good things we have done, so none of us can boast about it." Romans 11:6 says, "Since it is through God's kindness, then it is not by their good works. For in that case, God's grace would not be what it really is—free and undeserved."

Not only does He give us this gift, He promises to keep doing His work within us as long as we are alive. "I am certain that God, who began the good work within you, will continue his work until it is finally finished on the day when Christ Jesus returns" (Phil. 1:6).

God knew my brother's heart. Dennis was seeking God, and I believe he accepted Jesus as his Lord and Savior. Matthew 7:7–8 promises that when we ask, seek, and knock, God will open the door to us.

The End comes

Dennis's final massive seizure occurred when he was at home alone. His body went into rhabdomyolysis, a serious medical condition that occurs when damaged muscle tissue releases proteins and electrolytes into the blood. His organs failed. He remained on life support for three days before we made the decision to remove it. On August 15, 2015, we gathered around him in the hospital as the nurse turned off the IV medication pumps and disconnected the ventilator. Once she unplugged everything, his body settled back in a posture of peace and rest.

We prayed and sang songs of praise as his spirit left this earth and entered into the arms of his loving Father. The beats on the monitor screen slowed to asystole (what most people refer to as flatlining). At last, his struggles were over. He was in heaven, with a Father who knew all about his pain and suffering but loved him so much that He sent His Son to die for him. Despite his many earthly failures, Dennis was redeemed.

I know he no longer suffers from pain and depression, but I miss my younger brother. I still look twice when a Harley roars past or when I glimpse a Native guy with a beard and bushy eyebrows. I know I will never see Dennis again on this earth, but my heart never gives up hope.

I want to be that way with Jesus—looking for Him expectantly, hopefully, and longingly in everyday life.

I can't wait for a longer gaze when my brother and I are reunited in heaven.

Chapter 13

A Course Correction

During my clinical year of PA school, I spent six months completing my family-practice rotation. The clinic was the perfect place to learn, and I enjoyed the experience. However, when I completed my training, the clinic didn't have an opening for a physician assistant. I had to go where work was available: a small town in the wheat fields of southern Washington.

Part of the agreement with my PA scholarship required working in a medically underserved area for two years. So I traveled 120 miles every Monday morning to work in a family-practice clinic. I returned home on Tuesday nights after work so I could help my family care for my elderly grandfather on Wednesdays. At the crack of dawn on Thursdays I traveled back to work, returning home on Friday afternoons. My husband cared for our son with help from my mother.

After eighteen months I hit a wall. I felt physically, mentally, and emotionally spent.

During this time, my relationship with my aunt fell apart. While it was painful to experience such separation from a family member, God used the circumstances to show me truth.

> **After 18 months I hit a wall.**

After two grueling years, my contract ended and I returned to Spokane. I found a position as a primary care PA in the state prison system. I learned a lot about the ugly side of human nature there. People were there for all sorts of brutal crimes, including murder, rape, robbery, and vehicular manslaughter.

Seven and a half years later, I escaped into the world of urgent-care medicine.

An Internal Struggle

My new job afforded me the opportunity to travel to Ethiopia. When I answered the call, I fully believed it was God providing through me for a people in a far-off land who needed Him. I was one of the lucky ones because I got to participate in His plans.

But this trip brought internal struggle I never expected. More than eight thousand miles from home, among a people I had only ever encountered through the pages of a book, my life came full circle.

I captured some of my emotion in my journal entry on March 10, 2018:

I grew up in a Native home during the 1970s, and the sentiments similar to those of an activist group were often openly expressed in my home. Both my father and my stepmother had lifelong negative experiences with prejudice directed toward them simply because they were Native American.

The evening of the first day in Turmi I recalled a Floyd Westerman song from my childhood. The lyrics talk about how anthropologists came to Indian Country like death and taxes—two inescapable woes. The song points out how the government set aside money to study this culture within a culture as one might photograph animals in the zoo. I had a heavy heart this morning as I listened to my team members' perceptions of what bothered them most regarding their experience among the Hamar people. Several struggled with our own act of paying money in exchange for an opportunity to photograph a select group of young women, likening it to prostitution. The men of the group chose these women to pose for us, and the consensus was the women would not likely benefit or receive any of the proceeds from the encounter. The exchange was perceived as the men "pimping" the women out for profit.

I see many parallels between Ethiopian culture and my Native culture. I believe this is a factor that plays into why God chose me to return to Ethiopia. While I do not live the old way, I was raised by traditional parents, and they would tell you being Indian is inside the heart, mind, and soul.

Because this is an integral part of who I am, I believe my experience in Turmi comes with a different appreciation than some of my American counterparts. As a visitor, an American tourist of sorts, I wanted pictures of this people group. This group is vastly different from what people see when they look at me, yet similar to the person I am deep within my heart. I found myself at odds with my own actions.

With internal struggle, I ultimately succumbed to the desire to capture every memory I could.

My mind flashed back to American tourists taking pictures of me as a child while we Native people celebrated our heritage dressed in traditional regalia at a powwow. I heard negative comments expressing how my people feel when this happens. I think about how this makes me feel today. Casting emotions aside, I unapologetically participated in open exploitation of the Hamar people as I too raised my lens to capture the experience for posterity. I had become one of the loathsome anthropologists Floyd Westerman spoke of in his song.

Uncomfortable Questions

If I, a Christian and a Native American woman, bear the guilt of objectifying human beings, how am I to expect others to behave any differently? I struggle with the balance of wanting to live out the Great Commission ... to reach souls for the kingdom of heaven, believing this is the reason I was called to come to Turmi. But is it wrong to also have a strong desire to preserve the traditions of a culture? Life experience illustrates we were all created differently; different is not synonymous with bad.

What does this mean to me? Am I like the paralyzed woman we encountered? She arrived on the back of a motorcycle, with a dramatic entry, as her

> With internal struggle, I ultimately succumbed to the desire to capture every memory I could.

friends carried her expectantly toward us, seemingly in hopes of a miracle. It reminded me of the story in Matthew 5:17–25, where Jesus healed the paralyzed man after his friends lowered him through the tiles in the roof. I prayed for that miracle, but the woman in our scenario didn't get up and walk.

Some postulated she may have embraced her disabling condition as a form of self-pity. I wondered if she'd just lived that way for so long, she simply lost hope. Perhaps she was protecting her heart by rejecting the possibility of healing as a form of emotional self-preservation. Two opposing perspectives.

As a Native American, am I holding on to over two hundred years of oppression? For me, the struggle exists because I walk the fence; I have learned to assimilate between cultures. This is a gift and a curse. It is a truth I have lived with my entire life. How do I resolve these feelings?

Why has God called me here to serve the people in this land? I see the similarities to those I grew up with, and it touches my heart in a way I cannot describe. Is this a call to serve my people at home? Perhaps. This is something I need to earnestly pray about.

> He did not make a mistake when he created me. I believe I was created for a unique purpose.

As the influx of foreigners increases, with such fascination and interest in the Hamar, I recognize a need to pray for the hearts of the people who venture to this beautifully untouched place, that they will be respectful of the culture. I need to pray about my own acceptance of what this all means to my life and for revelation and discernment of what God may be doing in my heart.

There are people back home who have dedicated their existence to preserving our dying culture and language. I foresee the potential that something similar could one day transpire here in Turmi. But I know God is sovereign. Even though man is imperfect and sinful, God has not lost control. He did not make a mistake when He created me. I believe I was created for a unique purpose. I want to be available to be used for His work, wherever that may be. He has revealed my purpose—to serve people. I'm just not sure what that looks like at this moment. I have to remember Proverbs 19:21: "You can make many plans, but the Lord's purpose will prevail."

It absolutely amazes me to know that our God is alive and He answers prayer. When one of His children is hurting, He can and will heal us with a word; He etches understanding in our hearts. At this moment, my heart cries out the song "I Have Decided to Follow Jesus." There's no turning back for me!

Turn toward the Future

As I wrote those words in my journal, I cringed a little inside. I didn't want to work for Indian Health, but I thought God might have this in my future. Before that future arrived, though, it took numerous twists and turns.

Chapter 14

Painful Growth

The struggle and feelings I experienced in Turmi were no longer fresh in my mind; the rawness had softened. But God gently reminded me of this experience as I observed Him at work in my life, opening doors that had been closed by my circumstances. I watched, in awe, Him using all things together for good.

The story is like a jigsaw puzzle. The first piece originated with my participation in Bible Study Fellowship, an interdenominational, lay-led organization founded in 1959 by a British evangelist to China. Today thousands of groups meet weekly in 120 countries for a systematic exploration of God's Word, alternating between specific Old and New Testament books annually.

I wanted to grow in my faith, and without anyone holding my hand, I took a step and found a group in 2015, the year I first went to Ethiopia. After my second trip in 2018, I faded away for a while. God brought me back by unexpectedly placing the teaching leader in my direct path. When we reconnected, I confessed that although I had attended in the past, I had pretty much dropped out after my trip to Ethiopia.

Offering grace, she encouraged me to return. As my way of thanking her, I made a point to let her know she had made a difference in my life. This is not something I normally do; I am boisterous around people I know but quite shy otherwise. My tendency is to believe I am a mere minion, a peon, unworthy of attention or notice. But when God put her in my path, I developed a boldness I cannot explain.

The following year, she approached me and asked me to pray about leadership.

Who, me? I almost fell over but agreed to pray about it.

I rationalized that there were many reasons I was not equipped for service as a group leader. I'd been a Christian for years but a lazy one. My lack of Bible knowledge demonstrated that. Besides, I didn't possess the spiritual maturity needed to shepherd others. Group leaders were expected to make a commitment to attend weekly leadership meetings. They were responsible for ministering to a small group. I was keenly aware of how much I needed ministry myself. In addition, leaders met on Saturdays, and I worked every other Saturday.

No sooner had I decided that than God opened a door to a new job with a new schedule. I would be working Monday through Friday, with no more twelve-hour days or weekend shifts.

Pushed to a Decision

As soon as that opportunity arrived, I started receiving emails from a BSF leader. I wasn't sure who this person was; I get a lot of emails and don't always read them. But one caught my eye, because God had been urging me to have a difficult conversation with a friend that I didn't want to have. I'd prayed about it, and I knew I had to obey, but I was dragging my feet. When this email came, talking about having difficult conversations with friends, I asked myself, How does she know I'm faced with that very thing right now? I presumed God was speaking to me through her. He wanted me to share His truth with this friend, who was walking down a spiritually dangerous path.

> He wanted me to share his truth with this friend, who was walking down a spiritually dangerous path.

I obeyed God's nudge and had the difficult conversation, honoring God by setting my feelings aside. I allowed my words to reflect His truth rather than my judgment. She rejected me, which hurt, even though ultimately she was rejecting God. (I have faith that one day she will return to Him. It has been several years since we spoke, but when she returns to God, perhaps she will reach out to me.)

After I prayed about taking a leadership position with BSF, another email came from them, talking about passing the torch. It mentioned a retiring board member and contained a link to a blog. While I would not normally click on a link from a stranger, it intrigued me.

The blog talked about a medical physicist who grew up in Ghana. For some strange reason, God had planted an unexplainable love in my heart for Africa. This man told about how God had used BSF to deepen his relationship with the Lord and to strengthen his outreach work.

Then came the kicker. He said he viewed mentoring as a responsibility with far-reaching impact. He was challenged by Jesus's statement in Luke 12:48: "When someone has been given much, much will be required in return; and when someone has been entrusted with much, even more will be required."

This was the answer to my prayer. As much as the fear in me wanted to say no, I knew the answer was yes. God used what He knew would touch my heart to get my attention, and He used Scripture so I would know He was speaking to me.

More puzzle pieces were about to fall into place. Everything pointed to this new job serving Native people on the reservation where I once lived. It would be a change in many ways, starting with a fifty-mile drive each way. Instead of working three days a week, I would be required to work five.

Thrown a Curveball

I was ready to be used for God's glory on the reservation. I perceived this as His call on my life. I felt confident I'd made a strong impression during the interview. The door was about to open and I was ready to run through it. (Insert a hearty amen and hallelujah!)

But God doesn't always move as quickly as I want. After three months of waiting through background checks, fingerprinting, and completing a detailed questionnaire about grade school, high school, and every family member, they finally offered me the position. I was more than ready to go.

Then the unthinkable happened.

I noticed a subtle disfigurement in my left breast. There was no pain, lump, or discoloration, just a weird inversion that seemingly appeared overnight. At first I thought the fabric of my sports bras was compressing. But somewhere in the recesses of my brain, I recalled this as a presentation of breast cancer.

I had to tell someone! Unfortunately, my husband and I were heading to his hometown for his father's funeral. I didn't want to burden him.

Another Surprise

There was nothing I could do about it at that moment, so I said nothing. But my mind raced with unsettling thoughts. How could I tell my husband … my children … my employer?

How could I accept a new position when my future was so uncertain? I wouldn't have any paid time off for surgery or sickness caused by chemotherapy. Would I have access to short-term disability? Would I even qualify if the diagnosis came before the new position's start date? My whole world turned to chaos.

I asked God, Why now? Up until that moment I'd believed I was headed on the path He had planned for me. This storm left me no other option but to decline the offer.

As soon as I made the decision, I felt complete peace. I identified with the story of Abraham and Isaac in Genesis 22:6–13, where God directed Israel's

> **Unfortunately, my husband and I were heading to his hometown for his father's funeral.**

patriarch to sacrifice his only son. Only after Abraham laid Isaac on the altar and prepared to slay him did God stop the proceedings. "Don't lay a hand on the boy!" the angel said. "Do not hurt him in any way, for now I know that you truly fear God. You have not withheld from me even your son, your only son" (v. 12).

Was I to consider my left breast a sort of "burnt offering"?

As it turned out, after a mammogram, an ultrasound, and a visit to a surgeon, my primary care doctor determined it was likely the compression of my sports bra that had disfigured me, not cancer.

I believe God allowed this health scare to happen. He knew I would have accepted the position, because I thought it was what He wanted me to do. I trust Him with my future because—as this book's title says—He has His hand on me. He knows I want to be obedient to Him.

Leadership Role

As it turned out, I was not eligible for the local BSF leadership role because of my inability to attend meetings regularly. But God had that under control as well.

The woman who had been leading the online leaders' group was leaving, creating an opening for that position. Online group leaders could attend Zoom meetings that worked with their schedules. So that's what I did. For a year I participated in an international online group, which proved perfect for me. Learning how to host a Zoom meeting prepared me for leadership during the year of COVID-19 lockdowns, when meetings of every kind moved online.

I also began attending an evening Bible study with a group from another church. Through that study, God revealed to me the ugliness of my sin. It became an amazing time of spiritual growth.

One of the study's exercises called for us to recognize the strongholds in our lives, to confess that we gave them a foothold, and renounce them. I recognized many: pride, bitterness, and control, which had contributed to my mistreatment of others in the workplace. God revealed to me my negative attitude at work and helped me change it, molding me into a better person and a better provider.

At the right time God allowed me to read comments made by staff members at work on my performance review. While I had them in my possession, I had never taken the time to look at them. When I read descriptions of me as "the workplace bully"—an assessment written by more than one person—I cringed. The words stung, but I knew they were the truth.

God identified three people He wanted me to make amends with by

> When I read descriptions of me as "the workplace bully"- an assessment written by more than one person- I cringed.

apologizing for my behavior. I chose to embrace His nudge. I want my life legacy to point others to Jesus. But I knew if I were to die that day, there would have been people who said, "She was a Christian? Really?"

I cannot change the past, but I can learn from it. When God humbles me and asks me to apologize, I do it. Why? Because I know Peter's pain when he heard the rooster crow.

Seeking Forgiveness

When I encountered the three people God identified, I apologized with deep sincerity and asked them to forgive me for being mean to them. And they did.

God used my shortcomings for His glory.

There was a reason that Indian Health job was not for me: I had something worse than cancer that God wanted to heal. My willingness to allow Him to do that work in me allowed love to prevail, and He changed my heart.

This painful spiritual growth is one reason I find considerable inspiration in the words of the prophet Jeremiah:

> I know the plans I have for you," says the Lord. "They are plans for good and not for disaster, to give you a future and a hope. In those days when you pray, I will listen. If you look for me wholeheartedly, you will find me. I will be found by you," says the Lord. "I will end your captivity and restore your fortunes. I will gather you out of the nations where I sent you and will bring you home again to your own land. (Jeremiah 29:11–14)

As repentance and grace replaced my sadness, remorse, shame, and guilt, God placed a song of comfort in my heart. The song "Only Jesus" by Casting Crowns reminds us that the world encourages us to make a name for ourselves, but the only name that matters is Jesus.

Our time on earth is short. We are called to live for Jesus and leave a legacy that points to Him.

Chapter 15

Health Scares

"Faith shows the reality of what we hope for; it is the evidence of things we cannot see." (Heb. 11:1)

There's one thing that could shake me up as badly as my breast cancer scare: a crisis with my husband. In 2019, we arose at 4:30 in the morning to drive to the surgical center for two serious procedures. We arrived at his check-in time of 6:00, both bleary-eyed after not having slept much.

Brad and I prayed together before we entered the surgical center, where he would undergo a lumbar hemilaminectomy and micro-discectomy. That mouthful of medical terms refers to one procedure aimed at enlarging the space in the spinal column and another to treat a herniated disc. The goal was to relieve the pressure on a nerve that had been causing pain in his left hip and radiating into his left leg.

Over the past two weeks, my husband had been experiencing heart palpitations. The fluttering sensations in his chest became almost constant as his surgical date neared. The pre-ventricular contractions were frequent enough to stir up fear since every one of his father's brothers died prematurely of sudden cardiac death.

A quiet man of few words, Brad is a worrier, but you would never know it.

He got in to see his primary care provider right away. The doctor performed an electrocardiogram, which confirmed the arrhythmia. That brought an immediate referral to a cardiologist to determine whether it was safe to proceed with general anesthesia and surgery. Brad underwent more thorough studies, including another ECG and a stress. By late Friday afternoon, the physician cleared him for surgery on Monday morning.

Window of Opportunity

Recognizing all too clearly the potential risks associated with anesthesia and surgery, I might have been filled with fear. But the morning of the surgery I declared, "Not today, Satan!" My time in God's Word had given me fresh, new, bold faith. I knew that no matter what happened that day, God was in complete control.

As always, His timing was perfect. Even as they wheeled Brad into surgery, I smiled in the confidence of knowing the Author and Perfector of my faith was near, so I had nothing to fear. I stood on the truth of Ephesians 3:12: "Because of Christ and our faith in him, we can now come boldly and confidently into God's presence."

Every place I looked that day I found encouragement from God. I could trust the one who created the heavens and the earth, the loving God who sacrificed His only Son, and the Great Physician who took time out to meet with me that morning.

He saw my husband through surgery without any complications. The surgeon was blessed with supernatural precision. I stood on the mountaintop, singing God's praises, because He is so worthy of praise.

What might have overwhelmed me in chaos and struggle instead drew me closer to God. The experience strengthened my faith and contributed further to my testimony. God sees me, and His hand is on my husband as well.

The Battle Resumes

Unfortunately, victory in one episode doesn't mean you won't face another battle in the future. Two years after Brad's surgery, he developed cold symptoms, which intensified over the next twenty-four hours. He got tested for COVID-19. While we waited for the results, we prepared for the worst. We had no idea what was to come.

I read a phrase online that went something like "God has allowed you to be alone so you will reach out to Him." This stuck with me, even though I was not feeling particularly lonely at the time. The meaning surfaced all too clearly when several days later my husband tested positive for coronavirus.

Brad moved to the other side of the house to sleep in the spare bedroom. As uncomfortable as it made us feel, we wore masks in our home. I got tested too, but my results were negative. I remained asymptomatic as I watched my husband from a distance accepting the popsicles, sports drinks, and chicken soup I provided to replenish the electrolytes in his body.

I continually asked God to heal him. In my isolation, made worse by societal paranoia over COVID, I experienced a heavy, almost stifling sense of loneliness.

Angry and frightened, I sank in the waves amid a full-on hurricane, so overwhelmed I couldn't even reach out to Jesus. I called a few close friends. Some didn't recognize my desperation. Others had busy lives that pulled them in other directions.

It seemed like everyone had become desensitized to the problems of others. Those who knew we were vaccinated figured Brad would pull through fairly easily. But I was losing confidence, and I couldn't share my fears with anyone, least of all my husband. I had to remain strong for him. I cried on my way to work and alone in my bed at night.

While people complained about the vaccination mandate in our state, I wondered when my husband would turn the corner. Every day I asked how he was feeling. He always said he thought he was feeling a little better. But he lost twelve pounds and couldn't stop coughing. One time he nearly passed out in the shower and then again while sitting on the toilet.

I heard on television about some people who had lost loved ones to the disease. The family member was there one day and gone the next. The health-care provider in me mentally checked out. I feared the worst.

Blessings of Prayer

Without the support of friends or family, my morale continued to sink. I called a woman from my Bible study group and asked for prayer. She prayed this for me:

Heavenly Father, I lift Kim to You right now, asking that You wrap Your loving arms around her. Fill her with Your calm assurance. You've got this. You are sovereign. Nothing escapes Your watchful eye. Take Kim's fear. Bind the evil one and stop him from speaking fear into

Kim's heart. Help her to take captive those thoughts and refute them with who You are. God, fill Kim with Your peace. In Jesus's name, amen.

She reminded me that the Bible tells us to bear one another's burdens and to pray for one another, so it was okay for me to reach out. Then she prayed for my husband.

Heavenly Father, I lift Brad up to You, asking that You heal him. We don't know why You've allowed him to get sick, and why for so long, especially after being vaccinated. But we know each of our lives is in Your hands. We have zero control. You are a good, good Father. Help Brad's faith to grow as he faces all the uncertainties by leaning into who You are. Thank You for Your Word that speaks life and truth into us. In Jesus's name, amen.

The simple act of her taking time out of her day to pray for Brad and me changed my attitude. God had allowed me to be alone so I would seek Him. When I couldn't get there on my own, He placed a Christian friend in my path to point me to Him. She not only prayed but also offered Scripture to encourage me, including Philippians 4:6–7: "Don't worry about anything; instead, pray about everything. Tell God what you need and thank him for all he has done. Then you will experience God's peace, which exceeds anything we can understand. His peace will guard Your hearts and minds as you live in Christ Jesus." And Deuteronomy 31:8: "Do not be afraid or discouraged, for the Lord will personally go ahead of you. He will be with you; he will neither fail you nor abandon you."

> She reminded me that the Bible tells us to bear one another's burdens and to pray for one another, so it was OK for me to reach out.

The thirteen months Brad was off work were quite challenging. During one of my darkest hours, God came through for me unexpectedly through a friend. He allowed me to sit in my loneliness for a reason, but He was glorified through it. He used my loneliness and feelings of abandonment to teach me to be compassionate and caring. He taught me one of the fundamentals of the Christian faith, as demonstrated by Jesus's death on the cross: love means doing what is best for another, no matter the cost.

God also called me to show grace and forgiveness to the ones I felt had failed me. After all, He allowed the storm in my life for a reason. He was healing my husband and keeping His hands on both of us. This experience emphasized the truth of James 1:22–25:

> Don't just listen to God's word. You must do what it says. Otherwise, you are only fooling yourselves. For if you listen to the word and don't obey, is like glancing at your face in a mirror. You see yourself, walk away, and forget what you look like. But if you look carefully into the perfect law that sets you free, and if you do what it says and don't forget what you heard, then God will bless you for doing it.

Continuing Symptoms

Seven months after my husband was diagnosed with COVID-19, he continued to experience a rapid heart rate, a common problem with "long COVID," where symptoms can linger for weeks, months, or even years. Other

> God also called me to show grace and forgiveness to the ones I felt had failed me.

symptoms include shortness of breath, fuzzy thinking, and fatigue. His heart rate remained around 106 at rest, compared to a normal rate of 80. When he took a shower or walked across a parking lot, it accelerated to 140. His constant coughing caused a disc in his lumbar spine to protrude, pressing on one of his nerves and leaving him with constant leg pain. He underwent a series of epidural steroid injections, but the pain was unrelenting.

Brad couldn't mentally process information like he did in the past, and consequently he couldn't return to work. His job required mental sharpness; a lapse in judgment on his part could literally result in loss of life. He felt overwhelmed, defeated, and depressed. He lost twenty pounds, along with his sense of taste and smell for about nine months. He finally saw a cardiologist, who prescribed a beta blocker that returned his heart rate to normal.

At the depth of his despair, Brad told me he felt like he had turned into an old man. He wondered if he would ever be the same again. COVID had changed him, as it did all of us. Still, he was alive. At a time when all hope seemed lost, God reminded me of that truth during my daily Bible reading.

Jesus, full of the Holy Spirit, returned from the Jordan River. He was led by the Spirit in the wilderness, where the devil tempted Him for forty days. Jesus ate nothing all that time and became very hungry.
Then the devil said to him, "If you are the Son of God, tell this stone to become a loaf of bread."
But Jesus told him, "No! The Scriptures say, 'People do not live by bread alone.'
Then the devil took him up and revealed to him all the kingdoms of the world in a moment of time. "I will give you the glory of these kingdoms and authority over them," the devil said, "because they are mine to give to anyone I please." (Luke 4:1–6)

God allowed the devil to lead Jesus to a place to be sorely tempted. The devil had to have permission, and Jesus walked only where God allowed Him to walk. I knew that Brad and I were also walking through difficult times only because God had allowed it. Soon after this, during a daily reading as I sat across from my husband, God blessed me with Psalm 27:1–3:

The Lord is my light and my salvation—so why should I be afraid?
The Lord is my fortress, protecting me from danger, so why should I tremble?
When evil people come to devour me, when my enemies and foes attack me, they will stumble and fall.
Though a mighty army surrounds me, my heart will not be afraid.
Even if I am attacked, I will remain confident.

My husband's life looks very different than it did when all this began, but he is still alive. That is a blessing that I will never again take for granted.

Chapter 16

God Is Always Working

I haven't always been the nicest person. Even after becoming a Christian, I had problems controlling my tongue. This fault of mine gave birth to sin. I recently experienced the consequences and received the Lord's discipline. But it is within His loving discipline that we do some of our most profound growth.

I knew I had a problem. That was made very clear to me as I sat in my supervisor's office early one January day. I brought my frustrations to her after some recurrent staff issues had surfaced over the weekend. They resulted in inconvenience for one patient, unnecessary waiting for another, and improper discharge for another. I became so frustrated I raised my voice at the offending staff member. In my angst, I withheld nothing, fully expressing my frustration and disappointment with her lapse in judgment.

> **I recently experienced the consequences and received the Lord's discipline.**

Others within earshot were appalled, and they emailed my supervisor to let her know about my poor behavior.

As I sat in my office that day, God humbled me and allowed me to see the error of my ways. I repented for my outward display of anger toward another human being. In the parking lot at the end of the day, I prayed with sincerity and read Scripture, including Hebrews 12:4–11, which reminded me that none of us has given our lives in our struggle against sin, like Jesus did.

I read Proverbs 3:11–12, a reminder to not make light of God's discipline, because the Lord disciplines those whom He loves. If He didn't, we'd be like illegitimate children. If we respect our earthly fathers who discipline us, the writer asks, shouldn't we submit even more to the Father of our spirits?

In Hebrews 12, the writer concludes with this: "Our earthly fathers disciplined us for a few years, doing the best they knew how. But God's discipline is always good for us, so that we might share in his holiness. No discipline is enjoyable while it is happening—it's painful! But afterward there will be a peaceful harvest of right living for those who are trained in this way" (vv. 10–11).

I went into my meeting with my heart ready to accept whatever came my way. Instead of attempting to argue my case, I shared my concerns but owned my own failure and repented of my actions. I humbly accepted my well-deserved discipline.

My supervisor advised me a letter would follow; it would become part of the permanent record in my file. When the letter arrived in the mail a few days later, I knew what it was without opening it. The devil had been tormenting me with my failure. I was so filled with disgrace I couldn't even read it.

Full of guilt

When my husband saw the unopened letter sitting on the countertop a few days later, he asked about it. I told him it was the letter I'd been expecting from work. "You can read it if you want, but I'm not going to and I don't want to talk about it." I still felt too guilt-ridden and shame-filled to face it.

As I prayed fiercely, submitting to God's perfect will for my life, He revealed to me what I had to do. Faith, repentance, and love require action. It's not enough to profess our faith if we refuse to act on it. Repentance means we turn from our sin and follow a different path. We must move toward the person we are loving and show them our love, whether by providing for a need with a tangible gift or picking someone up when they fall. Blessing people

> ## My situation at work suddenly took a profound turn for the worse.

with words does not demonstrate our love or our faith. I was being called to demonstrate my faith, repentance, and Christ's love by apologizing to three people at work I had wronged. Talk about humbling.

God revealed to me who I needed to address and provided the moment of opportunity with each one. All I had to do was obey. This is what it means to "bear our own cross," a term I'd heard many times but never completely understood. We die to self when we submit to the Father's will. I chose His will and obeyed. And when I apologized with heartfelt sincerity, each one graciously forgave me.

Since that time, I have enjoyed good relationships with each of them. My demeanor at work changed. I began to enjoy my job again, and I realized a newfound appreciation for the staff. I also developed an appreciation for the truth of 1 John 4:4: "You belong to God, my dear children. You have already won a victory over those people, because the spirit who lives in you is greater than the spirit who lives in the world."

Change in the Air

After Barack Obama's historic election as the nation's first Black president, he made this profound statement during his acceptance speech: "This victory alone is not the change we seek; it is only the chance for us to make that change." I had been given the chance to make a change. I had grown. But a few months later I experienced another major change.

> I could do it, and nobody would find me until I was gone.

My situation at work suddenly took a profound turn for the worse. As I desperately searched for a new job, I clung to the truth of Genesis 50:20: what the enemy means for harm, God will often use for good.

As I walked through the refining fire of my situation, God led me to the powerful message in James 3:1–10 about taming the tongue. If we could control our tongues, we would be able to control ourselves in every other way. Like a small bit can guide a large horse, a small rudder turn a ship in any direction, or a tiny spark start a forest fire, so too can the small tongue create a world of wickedness and set our lives on fire, James says. "People can tame all kinds of animals, birds, reptiles, and fish, but no one can tame the tongue. It is restless and evil, full of deadly poison" (vv. 7–8).

In the past my tongue had been full of poison. Feeling broken and defeated, I developed a headache that went on for three weeks. I felt as if I were in the midst of flames I couldn't extinguish. Through it, however, I learned that God's work in me was not yet complete.

Because of the events that transpired during that time, I harbored bitterness, anger, and resentment for several months. I held on to malice and a desire to seek revenge. The enemy used my circumstances to try to disable me and to destroy my witness. But God had other plans.

During this troubling time of stress and angst, I wrestled with God. One minute my heart would soften, but the next minute I turned angry and resentful. I was grabbing hold of my sin and letting it go repeatedly, all day long, on a daily basis.

Battle with Bitterness

In one dark moment, as I sat in my office alone between patients, a vision came to me. In my anger, bitterness, self-loathing, and malice, I envisioned myself hanging from the hook on the back of the office door, dead by my own hands. A gruesome thought invaded my mind: I could do it, and nobody would find me until I was gone.

Thankfully, my merciful, loving, and compassionate God fully embraced me at that very moment. He showed me grace and intervened. He opened a door for me, releasing me from the enemy's strongholds. I realized my identity was not defined by my temporary circumstances. I claimed victory in the name of Jesus. Jesus defines my identity. I am a child of God, and the enemy has no control over me.

God allowed me to leave a legacy of forgiveness and restoration among many of the people I worked with as evidence of the life-changing fruit of the grace and forgiveness Jesus showed me on the cross. I let go of my sin and allowed God to demonstrate His unfailing love through me. This is what I am called to do.

> I can now step into and out of the fiery furnace, fully appreciating the gravity of what it means to be surrounded by fire.

Showing more of Him and less of me is an exercise in dying to self. He empowers me with his Holy Spirit to accomplish what I cannot do in my own strength. With God, all things are possible. As Jesus faced death by crucifixion, in His human servant form, He prayed, "Father, if you are willing, please take this cup of suffering away from me. Yet I want your will to be done, not mine" (Luke 22:42).

And then He died. He gave His life for me, a sinner—not because I deserved it or because of who I am but because of who He is. He asked me to do things that were uncomfortable to help me grow. Through my obedience, He blessed me.

I thought of the story in the book of Daniel, where a furious King Nebuchadnezzar ordered Shadrach, Meshach, and Abednego thrown into a furnace at a temperature seven times hotter than usual. The outcome was completely different from what the king expected because God, who is much bigger than any earthly leader, demonstrated He had other plans for these three men.

When the king looked into the furnace and saw a fourth person walking in the blazing fire with them and then witnessed them coming out of the furnace untouched by the flames, he said,

"Praise to the God of Shadrach, Meschach, and Abednego! He sent his angel to rescue his servants who trusted in him. They defied the king's command and were willing to die rather than serve or worship any god except their own God" (Daniel 3:28). God changed King Nebuchadnezzar's heart in an instant.

Emerging from Ashes

God had allowed me to walk through the fire too. And He sent an angel to be with me. I emerged from the ashes, and though my outward appearance is unchanged, inwardly I am stronger. I can now step into and out of the fiery furnace, fully appreciating the gravity of what it means to be surrounded by fire. I know fire can be consuming, but I also know it can refine me. I can come through the flames gleaming.

Zechariah 13:9 says, "I will bring that group through the fire and make them pure. I will refine them like silver and purify them like gold. They will call on my name, and I will answer them. I will say, 'These are my people,' and they will say 'The LORD is our God.'"

I have come through a season of testing, but I have not been thrown away. God's Word says, "We know that God causes everything to work together for the good of those who love God and are called according to his purpose for them" (Rom. 8:28).

The entire time I walked in the furnace, God had a hand on me. I have stepped into a new job, and things are good. My outlook is different, and my future is promising. I am blessed.

I have been appointed an opportunity to care for people who suffer from chronic pain, a condition I well understand. As I learn and grow into the healer God has called me to be, I rely on His grace and mercy in new ways. When I find myself in unfamiliar waters, when it's all I can do at times just to tread water, when I feel myself sinking, I may feel frightened at times, but I have an underlying sense of peace. I know I am right where God has me for a reason. I want to be a beacon in someone's darkness for God.

A year later, when God knew my heart was ready, He opened a door that allowed complete healing and closure regarding the circumstances that led up to my leaving my position in the urgent care facility. He replaced my bitterness and shame with forgiveness and redemption. He kept me in His loving embrace, and through my willing heart, He restored a relationship broken by pride. He is a God of second chances and He completes every good work.

Now more than ever I need His protection.

Chapter 17

An Orphan's Legacy

The pandemic didn't just affect my husband's health. COVID-19 turned my world upside down and left me feeling like an orphan. Amid lockdown fever, riots occurring after a Black Lives Matter event, and the enemy's presence on social media, a seemingly cataclysmic divide occurred in my family relationships.

In circumstances like this, I must desperately cling to my Father in heaven, who promises to never leave me or forsake me.

My father and I didn't speak for years. We were separated by my rebellion and disobedience and his pain over my adolescent choices that seemed to destroy any dreams he had for the person I was meant to be. But one day at my sister's house, I knelt in front of him, crying and apologizing. He forgave me. We reconciled and restored the loving bond between father and daughter.

This relationship parallels my relationship with my Father in heaven.

When I was eighteen, I wrote a song for my dad. He has never seen it.

I haven't said a word to my daddy in so long.
I didn't quite know how, so I wrote him this song.
About my life ...
Well, I'm doing just fine.
My baby is two now. Come and see her sometime.
I hope you can forgive me for all that I've done.
'Cause I wanna be friends with the best daddy under the sun.

I never learned to write music, but if I had, those lyrics would have been sung to a country-western tune.

With all that I have done to disappoint my father, getting married at sixteen may have been the worst blow. I appreciated his pain when my own daughter made the decision to leave our home at seventeen.

> With all that I have done to disappoint my father, getting married at sixteen may have been the worst blow. I appreciated his pain when my own daughter made the decision to leave our home at seventeen.

Before my grandfather died, I spent every Wednesday with him for about a year and a half. During those visits he told me my grandmother did something similar after the two of them met one summer while working in the cherry orchards in the state of Washington. She had traveled there with her family, but when it came time for her to return home, she told my grandpa she wanted to go with him. That's what she did. They married and remained together until Grandma died in her sixties at the hands of a drunk driver. My grandfather spent the next thirty years alone. He was in his final years when he shared their story with me.

So leaving home and getting married at a young age has spanned the generations in our family.

Generational Abandonment

My father shared with me a story about his mother sending him a "Dear John" letter when he was drafted during the Korean War. During that same time, my mother sent him her version as well. After being abandoned in a foreign country, when he returned home, not one person showed up to welcome him at the bus station. Just thinking about that saddens me.

In Genesis 30, Rachel and Leah both longed to bear a child. Their desire became more important to them than God or their relationship with their shared husband, Jacob.

Personal pain often shows up in the relationships that are closest to us. Our pain blinds us to God's truths and we may hurt others as a result. My family has a history of abandonment.

My father was essentially raised by his grandmother. When he was a boy, his parents often left him on her farm, surrounded by wheat field fields on the Coeur d'Alene Reservation. When he was older, his parents sent him to boarding school, which was not a good experience. As an adult he could not understand why his parents left him so much of the time. He couldn't make sense of it or the emotional and psychological wounds he bore as a result. My dad experienced abandonment by people he should have been able to trust.

My mother also knew physical and emotional abandonment. At a time when divorce was rare, her father's infidelity ended his marriage to my grandmother. He deserted her and their three young daughters, and Grandma raised them without a father's loving guidance or provision.

When I was in first grade—the same age as my mother when her father left— she left my older sister, me, my little brother, and my father to begin a new life with my stepfather. The cycle continued.

> I no longer have to lash out in anger with a desire to inflict pain where pain has been inflicted on me, because my God is the God of peace.

Time and time again, members of my family have been wounded by physical and emotional abandonment. The scars are not obvious to the outside world, but people can plainly observe the physical absence. Both forms burden a person with the deep wounds of shame, guilt, and a sense of loss that cuts all the way to the heart. The flesh may heal, but the underlying damage manifests as an indescribable angst. It can result in addiction, isolation, depression, bitterness, and collateral damage that wounds anyone in its path.

Diamonds from Dust

I became a great-grandmother at age fifty-seven. I prefer to be called GiGi instead of Great-Grandma, but I am accepting the reality that I am aging.

But this is not the definition of who I am, because my story was ultimately written by the Ruler and Creator of the universe. While the pieces may look like a complete mess, God makes diamonds out of dust. He creates beauty from ashes. With God, all things work together for good. What the enemy means for harm, God can turn around for His glory, which is what Joseph told his brothers in Genesis 50:20.

Disaster has led me to the deepest of valleys as well as the highest of mountaintops. Because God has His hand on me, I refuse to reach for the hand of a liar or imposter. My Father is the King of the universe. I am a child of God. I am not alone. I am called to obey the God of peace!

Through these experiences, I have learned the truth that God will never leave me or forsake me. When fears of abandonment and rejection hit me like a storm, He is with me in the midst of it. If I look up and say, "Jesus, save me," His presence calms me and He leads me through my circumstances.

How I respond to my circumstances looks much different today. I no longer have to lash out in anger with a desire to inflict pain where pain has been inflicted on me, because my God is the God of peace. I don't have to let pride prevent me from being humble, because in Jesus's humility I have been blessed with life everlasting. He is creating His story in my life. I am no longer who I used to be because God has His hand on me. I am not walking through the storms alone because He is always with me.

Jesus is the Author and Perfecter of my faith. As I take each step forward, I walk with Him. I know He will take me places for the betterment of my life and the lives He has intertwined with mine. All I need to do is trust Him.

As we face life's storms, we can easily feel overcome by the wind and the waves. One moment we are sailing on what appears to be smooth waters in what feels like a sturdy vessel. At the next moment we're clinging to the remnants of a rapidly sinking, capsized boat. All appears hopeless as we're surrounded by dark clouds, with no land in sight. These storms can come in many forms: the loss of a job, a divorce, a diagnosis of cancer, a lost pregnancy, the death of a loved one, a betrayal. The world is full of challenges.

> She told me my father had had a major heart attack and been flown by helicopter to a hospital in Spokane.

When my husband contracted COVID-19, I felt the same sense of profound loneliness I experienced when my younger brother was on life support, just before he died. I remember that sense of desperation, knowing this was the end and there was nothing I could do to change the circumstances. In my anguish I reached out for human companionship, aching for someone to help me bear this overwhelming burden of grief. I came up empty. Emotionally abandoned by the people I wanted support from.

Uncertain Times

The pandemic lockdown, and the panic that continued long after as the virus morphed and several variants surfaced, wreaked havoc in many people's lives.

During this time, a careless comment on social media placed a wedge between my relationships with my father, my husband, and my sister. I stopped using my social media account, seeing it as the devil's playground. But these relationships appeared hopelessly damaged.

We went for more than a year without sharing more than a few texts. I hadn't given up, but aside from our limited conversations, I didn't see healing coming any time soon.

I reached out to my father during my darkest moments when I thought my husband was going to die, and he replied lovingly. But our relationship still seemed far from healed.

In September, as the new year for BSF studies began, my teaching leader asked us to write down a prayer for the group to pray. I asked for healing and restoration for my family. God answered in a way I never would have believed.

A month later, as I sat in my leader's meeting for BSF one Saturday morning, my stepmother called me. I didn't answer right away since at that moment I was sharing my gratitude for how God had placed one of the ladies unexpectedly in my life as an answer to prayer, how God used COVID-19 to help slowly rekindle my relationship with my father, and how my prayer for healing of a relationship that was so wounded might be starting to be answered.

I left the meeting and called her back. She told me my father had had a major heart attack and been flown by helicopter to a hospital in Spokane. I quickly went home and told my husband. The two of us made our way to the emergency room. By the time we arrived, my father was in the cath lab. Nobody was allowed in for hospital visits since coronavirus cases were on an upward trend. So for the next week we just waited and prayed.

We kept in close communication with my stepmother, and we took pajamas and slippers to the hospital to make my father's stay more comfortable. I made him a card with a picture of myself and my sister as children and wrote on it that I loved him.

On the day he was discharged, we met him at the front door. I cried as we embraced. He said, "My Kimmy Rae ... my Kimmy Rae." Once again, all was forgiven.

My Father in heaven restored my relationship with my father on earth. He used a heart attack, something the devil wanted to use for harm, and made diamonds out of dust.

Struggles Continue

After Dad's release from the hospital, we began spending Sundays with my parents in Coulee Dam—nearly ninety miles away from our house. My father started losing weight since he had no interest in food after his heart attack. His physical strength was dwindling as well.

When my stepmother mentioned the idea of moving to Spokane to be closer to us and their doctors, I wondered about multigenerational living in the same house. It seemed our relationship was healing, and living together could really make a difference for them since meal preparation had become difficult for my stepmother.

While we tossed the idea around, we traveled to Brad's hometown to spend Thanksgiving with his family. No sooner had the holiday ended than we found ourselves in crisis mode again. Brad's mother began feeling ill and showed signs of confusion, which was related to a urinary tract infection. That led to acute kidney failure and hospitalization. We thought we were going to need to bring her to our home for a while. She declined my husband's offer, telling him she was fine. We knew she was not fine, but we couldn't force her to come to our home.

> She didn't leave this world alone because God mercifully allowed her son to be there with her.

Shortly thereafter, she was released. We continued to visit my father and stepmother every weekend, but after the first of the year, Brad's mother developed an arterial clot in her leg, and Brad went back to be with her. A surgeon gave him options for his mother. The first was surgery, which she might not survive and would likely be so hard on her kidneys she would require dialysis for the rest of her life. The alternative: they could "keep her comfortable."

She was ready to go to battle with the Grim Reaper and chose to take her chances, so she elected to try surgery. The next morning the surgeon talked about discharging her from the hospital. Brad was dumbfounded! He told the surgeon, "Twenty-four hours ago you were talking about comfort care, and now you're saying she can go home?"

The surgeon couldn't explain it, but she was getting arterial blood flow to her leg and wouldn't require surgery. God answers prayers when the situation seems hopeless!

With both sets of our parents aging, we wondered who would be moving in with us first.

The Final Watch

In April we took time off from traveling to Coulee Dam while Brad went to visit his mother. He hadn't returned to work because of long COVID symptoms, so he was able to spend some time with her.

During that visit, the arterial clot recurred, and this time she didn't survive. Brad stayed with her in the hospital during her final days. He played hymns on his phone for her as he comforted her. She didn't leave this world alone because God mercifully allowed her son to be there with her. As painful as that experience was, he wouldn't have had it any other way.

He continued to love her by carrying out her wishes regarding her estate. Despite his physical and emotional pain, he saw that everything was done just as she wanted. God gave him the strength to do what he wouldn't have otherwise imagined being able to accomplish.

Brad remained off work for just over a year. Even now, he sometimes searches for words and tires easily. He will require surgery for the disc issue related to the cough. But he survived COVID-19, and for that I am grateful.

After months of discussion, we sold our home to buy a multi-generational dwelling to someday share with my parents or other family members who might need temporary assistance. If chaos suddenly ensues, we will be prepared. God worked out the details perfectly. When it comes to planning, He is always one step ahead of us.

Chapter 18

Not the Final Chapter

My day typically begins in the Word. One day I started weeping before the Lord as He spoke to me from the book of Genesis. I was reading the story of Joseph, who was sold into slavery by his brothers because of their envy of him. Joseph had shared his dream about being out in the field tying up bundles of grain when his bundle suddenly stood up and their bundles all gathered around and bowed low before his. He told them about another dream, where the sun, moon, and eleven stars bowed down to him.

His brothers hated him for these revelations. Unbeknownst to their father, they sold Joseph into slavery. His father was heartbroken when the brothers offered him a shred of Joseph's robe dipped in blood and allowed Jacob to believe a wild animal had devoured Joseph. Jacob grieved for years, refusing to be comforted.

But Joseph was favored by God. He became a personal attendant to Potiphar, captain of the guard to Pharaoh. Potiphar recognized the Lord was with Joseph, who gave him success in everything. Potiphar put Joseph in charge of his house with administrative responsibility over everything Potiphar owned. Joseph had no worries. But Potiphar's wife tried to seduce him. When Joseph refused her advances—literally running away from her and leaving his cloak in her hand—she used it against him and claimed he had tried to rape her.

> **Joseph was sent to prison for a crime he didn't commit, but the Lord's favor remained with him.**

Joseph was sent to prison for a crime he didn't commit, but the Lord's favor remained with him. Joseph became a favorite of the warden, who put him in charge of the other prisoners, including Pharaoh's chief cupbearer and chief baker, who were locked up when Pharaoh became angry with them. One night they both had troubling dreams, which Joseph interpreted for them.

The chief cupbearer fared well; the baker did not. Joseph asked the chief cupbearer to remember him before Pharaoh. Two years passed. When Pharoah needed his dreams interpreted, the cupbearer told him about Joseph.

With full dependence on God, Joseph interpreted Pharaoh's dreams. He told Pharaoh the seven healthy cows and healthy heads of grain represented seven years of prosperity. But, Joseph warned, the seven scrawny cows and thin heads of grain represented seven years of famine that would follow. "This famine will be so severe that even the memory of the good years will be erased. As for having two similar dreams, it means that these events have been decreed by God, and he will soon make them happen" (vv. 31–32).

Recognizing that Joseph was filled with the Spirit of God, Pharoah appointed him in charge of the entire land of Egypt, placed a signet ring on his finger, and gave him an Egyptian name and a wife. At the age of thirty, this Hebrew who had been sold into slavery now reigned over Egypt.

Joseph's predictions about the abundance and famine came to fruition. He stored grain during the good years, so they had plenty during the famine.

When Jacob heard about this, he sent his sons to Egypt to purchase grain so the family wouldn't die. All but the youngest, Benjamin (Joseph's only other full brother, born to Rachel), went. Jacob had already lost Joseph and could not bear to lose Rachel's other son.

When his brothers came to buy grain, Joseph recognized them but didn't let on. He recalled his dreams so many years ago, of their bundles bowing down to his bundles. He learned his father was still living and his brother Benjamin was also alive.

After hearing them discussing their guilt over selling him thirteen years earlier, Joseph wept privately. Then he showed them mercy, selling them grain but returning the money they paid him for it. He held their brother Simeon to ensure they would return with Benjamin, but Jacob refused to allow Benjamin to go, fearing he would lose him as well.

Time passed and the grain supply dwindled. Joseph's family was going to starve without more grain. Finally, Jacob succumbed and sent Benjamin back to Egypt, but told his sons to take back the extra money Joseph had returned to them.

> ## For once and for all, I needed to forgive my parents for the ugliness of my past.

Joseph had every right to despise his brothers. He could have tortured them, but he showed them mercy and forgiveness. He had an animal slaughtered for a feast with his brothers. Again, he had their sacks filled with grain, returning their money a second time, but this time he had his silver cup placed in Benjamin's bag. He told the palace manager to chase them down and reveal the "stolen" cup in Benjamin's bag, requiring Benjamin to return as his slave. Distraught, the brothers all returned.

Judah explained to Joseph the despair Jacob would have over the loss of his son Benjamin. The brothers could not bear the grief this would cause, knowing it would lead to his death. Judah offered himself in place of Benjamin.

Joseph sent his attendants away. When it was only Joseph and his brothers in the room, he revealed his identity. Joseph did not seek vengeance. He did not shame his brothers. To restore relationship with his family, he forgave them.

Hitting Home

After reviewing Genesis, I read Luke 22, where Jesus revealed to His disciples what was about to happen to Him. As they were arguing with one another about who was going to be the greatest among them, Jesus knew he was about to die. Judas, a disciple who'd walked the earth with Jesus, betrayed him with a kiss. And Peter, as Jesus predicted, betrayed Him by denying his relationship with Him three times. That familiar story pierced my heart once again.

I love how God uses what He knows will touch our hearts to speak to us. He is a personal God, and He used a Scripture near and dear to my heart to teach me a valuable lesson. It all came together for me, and my heart surrendered.

Joseph was willing to forgive crazy betrayal to restore the relationship with his family, despite his suffering. He recognized it was God's provision for his family during a time of hardship.

Jesus was willing to go to the cross to restore relationship with His family. We, His brothers and sisters, have been separated from our Father because of our sin. His death sentence, like Joseph's sentence of imprisonment, was for the good of His family. So with unfathomable grace, mercy, willingness, and humility, He went to the cross.

Suddenly knowing what I was being called to do, I wept. For once and for all, I needed to forgive my parents for the ugliness of my past. I needed to forfeit what I had long seen as my earned right to anger, unforgiveness, pain, and hurt. This wasn't about my perceived rights but about my relationship with God and obedience to what He was asking of me.

With tears streaming down my face, I sent my father a message:

I learned a valuable lesson this morning in my time with the Lord. I read about Joseph in the book of Genesis. The Joseph who was sold into slavery by his brothers after he shared his dreams about them all bowing down to him. God blessed Joseph, even in prison after his master's wife falsely accused him. Joseph had every reason to be angry and bitter. Years passed, and when Joseph became a great leader, his brothers bowed down to him. He could have harbored resentment, but he chose to forgive. His relationship with his family was more important to him than his pain from their betrayal.

> God allowed the unthinkable to happen so we could realize a complete healing where I didn't think it would ever be possible.

Then I read in Luke where Judas betrayed Jesus with a kiss, and Peter betrayed Jesus by denying he knew Him three times, but Jesus obediently went to the cross to restore relationships between God and His children. I am sorry I hurt you, Dad, on top of the lashing from others. I reacted out of pain, and it was wrong. I hope you can forgive me. I am letting go of my feelings of betrayal. I want to restore the family relationship. I love you.

Coming Together

God had been working on my heart for months, just as I had been working on obedience for months. This all came together in my morning time in the Bible. My obedience lifted a heavy weight from my heart. And just like that, I was healed. God lovingly and gently brought everything together through my time with Him. Had I not chosen to seek His heart during this time, I may have missed it.

Once again, God had a hand on me because of the faithfulness of Jesus and His willingness to unselfishly go to the cross for me. To me, it represented the fulfillment of His promise in Jeremiah 29:11–14 and His plans to give me a future and a hope.

My story isn't over. In a world of uncertainty, I can trust that God knows the ending. He knows what is coming, and He prepares our hearts for healing ... but not a moment too soon.

On October 9, two months after my husband was diagnosed with COVID-19, paramedics flew my father to Spokane by helicopter. After the Lord so graciously healed my wounded heart, my father suffered his heart attack. Through it, we were given a second chance to restore a relationship that had been wounded by the enemy. God allowed the unthinkable to happen so we could realize a complete healing where I didn't think it would ever be possible.

Some people might feel defeated by tragic events similar to what I described transpiring in my life. But I saw God do some of His best work during that time! Now I almost welcome suffering, because it is in the midst of suffering that we come face-to-face with God. That's why God told Paul, "My grace is all you need. My power works best in weakness." And why Paul responded, "Now I am glad to boast about my weaknesses, so that the power of Christ can work through me" (2 Cor. 12:9).

Generational Sin's Impact

During a year of faithfully meeting with God to study Genesis, I was able to clearly see the effects of generational sin. While I read the stories of Jacob and Esau in Genesis 32, I took a good look in the mirror. Several women in my Bible study commented that Jacob was not a nice person, as he selfishly deceived Esau out of his birthright and his blessing. But I thought, I am no better.

> **He will accomplish His will in our lives whether or not we accompany each other on the journey.**

Jacob praised God for the blessings He bestowed upon him, acknowledging that he was not worthy. Jacob asked God to remember His promises to him as he returned to the promised land. He asked for protection against his brother, because the last time he saw Esau twenty years earlier, Esau had threatened to kill him for stealing his blessing.

Jacob offered Esau a lavish array of gifts to appease him: two hundred female goats, twenty male goats, two hundred ewes, twenty rams, thirty female camels and their young, forty cows, ten bulls, twenty female donkeys, and ten male donkeys. He sent the herds and his herdsmen on ahead so Esau would pass all of them before he came to Jacob and his family. He instructed each herdsman to tell Esau the animals belonged to Jacob but were a gift for "his master, Esau."

The night before they were to meet with Esau, Jacob sent his wives, servant wives, and all his belongings to the other side of the Jabbok River. As he stayed behind alone, a man (God) came and wrestled with him all night long. God did not defeat Jacob, although he easily could have. When daybreak came, he touched Jacob's hip, wrenching it out of its socket. The Genesis 32:26–30 passage is one of the most dramatic in Scripture:

> The man said, "Let me go, for the dawn is breaking."
> But Jacob said, "I will not let you go unless you bless me."
> "What is your name?" the man asked.
> He replied, "Jacob."

"Your name will no longer be Jacob," the man told him. "From now on you will be called Israel, because you have fought with God and with men, and have won."

"Please tell me your name," Jacob said.

"Why do you want to know my name?" the man replied. Then he blessed Jacob there.

Jacob named the place Peniel (which means "face of God"), for he said, "I have seen God face to face, yet my life has been spared."

As everything came together in my understanding of Scripture, I gained a view of myself in Jacob. I wrestle with God occasionally. I have been deceptive to get what I want, trusting my own shrewdness and strength to accomplish my will.

> Each one of us is like filthy rags, and none of us deserves God's grace. That's what makes the gift so amazing.

In the biblical story, God touched Jacob's hip, and Jacob limped as a result. This became a constant reminder to him that God is in control. For me that illustrated the biblical truth that His power is made perfect in our weakness. God healed Jacob and Esau's relationship, but Jacob did not follow Esau to Seir. Instead, Jacob went his own way to Shechem, where he built an altar to the God of Israel. God can heal relationships, but people may not come together afterward, and that's okay. That is God's message for me, I thought.

He will accomplish His will in our lives whether or not we accompany each other on the journey. I was willing to accept this might be my truth ... until my father's heart attack. God was beyond generous. In an overwhelming act of kindness and mercy, He provided complete healing and restoration of my relationship with my father. Now every Sunday my husband and I visit with my father and stepmother. God is so, so good.

As the story of healing continued to unfold before me, I remained in awe and wonder.

I recalled how Jesus asked the woman of Samaria for a drink from Jacob's well. I pictured myself as her as she ran back to the village shouting with joy, "Come and see a man who told me everything I ever did! Could he possibly be the Messiah?" (John 4:29).

My heart leapt with the joy of the Holy Spirit as I recognized my own sanctification.

As I was getting ready for work and listening to the notes of my Bible study lesson, God revealed His truth in me. Everything I had been living was knit together in that moment. I felt absolutely overwhelmed. I got into my car and drove to work, made new with God's mercy for the day, on the verge of tears.

A song called "Scars," performed by the group I Am they, came on the radio. I listened as if hearing it for the first time. The lyrics took on new meaning, and I was overcome with emotion. The song is about the scars from the nails Jesus bore for humanity in His darkest hour. The writer professes his thankfulness for Jesus's scars and says he would not know God's heart without them. It's true.

We only come to know how much God loves us when we fully grasp the enormity of what it means that He was willing to sacrifice His only Son to atone for our sins. The writer of this song identifies his own darkest hour as the moment when he finally came to the end of himself. That happens for many of us. When we have nowhere to turn, we fall to our knees in prayer, looking for an answer. And God never fails us.

That day, this song took on new meaning for me. As I sang along, I thought about my own scars, which brought me to Jesus. All the wounds I have incurred during my life are part of my story. God has a purpose for every one of them. Even though He does not choose our wounds, He allows them to happen and He will use them all for His good.

When I got to work, I shared my story with a friend, sobbing. I had been wrecked by God, and through it, He blessed my day. I am nobody special. But God has His hand on me. And if God is for me, who can be against me?

I hope my stories have offered you hope in a God who sees everything … a God who knows your innermost secrets and loves you so much He sent His Son to die for you.

Life is short, and none of us is promised another day. If this was your last day on earth, would you die knowing you are going to heaven? If not, you can!

It's simple. All you have to do is accept God's free gift of grace. No matter what you've done, He loves you and wants a relationship with you.

Each one of us is like filthy rags, and none of us deserves God's grace. That's what makes the gift so amazing.

If you have never accepted it before but would like to do so now, pray the prayer below:

Dear Lord God, I know I am a sinner and I need a Savior. I want to turn away from my sinful life to the life You have planned for me. I ask for Your forgiveness. Please cleanse me of my past and make me new. I believe Your Son, Jesus, died for me. I believe in my heart that You raised Him from the dead. I accept, confess, and proclaim Jesus Christ as my personal Lord and Savior. I invite Him to live in my heart from this day forward. Thank You, Jesus, for Your grace that has saved me from my sins and given me eternal life. Please send Your Holy Spirit to guide me and help me do Your will for the rest of my life. In Jesus's name, amen.

Hallelujah! The angels are rejoicing!

ORDER INFORMATION

To order additional copies of this book, please visit
www.redemption-press.com.

Also available at Christian bookstores
and Barnes & Noble.